# PILGRIM ON A BICYCLE

# PILGRIM ON A BICYCLE

Coast to coast in search of community

**BARBARA MARY JOHNSON**

CHRISTIAN HERALD BOOKS
Chappaqua, New York

Library of Congress Cataloging in Publication Data

Johnson, Barbara Mary.
    Pilgrim on a bicycle.

    Summary: The author describes her experiences with a group of Christians
bicycling across the United States.
    1. Bicycle touring — United States.    2.  United States — Description and
travel — 1960-    .    [1. Bicycles and Bicycling.    2. United States — Description
and travel.    3.  Christian life]  I. Title.
GV1045.J63          917.3          81-68637
ISBN 0-86693-001-9 (pbk.)          AACR2

**MEMBER OF
EVANGELICAL CHRISTIAN
PUBLISHERS ASSOCIATION**

Christian Herald, independent, evangelical and interdenominational, is dedicated
to publishing wholesome, inspirational and religious books for Christian families.

First Edition
CHRISTIAN HERALD BOOKS, 40 Overlook Drive, Chappaqua, New York 10514
Printed in the United States of America

"Dedicated to a community of pedaling pilgrims"

# Contents

# PILGRIM ON A BICYCLE

# 1

# One Way to Go

**I** PANICKED. I was so startled by that first meeting with our fellow bicyclists that I forgot to look at the ocean, breathe in that salty, wonderful damp air of the beach, or listen to the gulls shrieking overhead.

But I did check Ted's face to see what his first impressions were. I could see his eyebrows form a horizontal line over silver-rimmed eyeglasses. The rest of his face was masked by moustache and beard.

The two of us were on a Pacific beach in Lincoln City, Oregon, population 4198, with a party of 29 diverse people ready to set out the next morning on a coast-to-coast, cross-country bicycle trip. The assembled group did not look like transcontinental bikers to me. But, to be honest, neither did Ted or I, and I seriously doubted that we all would pedal into Hampton Beach, New Hampshire, seven-and-a-half weeks later, as planned.

And there was another goal to attain; we hoped to form a caring, sharing Christian community on wheels. Could we do it? Could a group of self-centered strangers from diverse back-grounds and lifestyles tolerate and respect each other enough to become mature brothers and sisters in Christ?

This cross-country bicycle trip was my big dream, one that I had convinced Ted to share with me. Would we both be sorry? I really couldn't feel very positive about biking companions who were fat — one young man was as round as a beach ball — or those who appeared weak and lethargic. Ted and I had pictured the group quite differently when we had received our official list of participants.

We had signed up with Out-Spokin's bike hike because the outfit's proposed coast-to-coast trip offered what we wanted — so we thought. There would be a van and trailer to carry gear, and bikers' ages ranged from sixteen to sixty-five. My fifty-first birthday was right before the trip, and Ted's fifty-second would occur on the trip, somewhere in South Dakota, so we fit well into the range.

"There could be plenty of bikers even older than we are," I said. "It sounds to me like it's quite a diverse group."

After we signed up, we received the list of participant names, followed by a comma and each biker's age. We discovered that the next closest to us in age was only twenty-six. There weren't any bikers in their thirties; none in their forties; and certainly nobody in their sixties. There were just the two of us, standing alone in our fifties, looking out of place on that pink, mimeographed sheet.

"They're all babies," Ted said as he studied the list. "Looks like you picked a young crowd."

"Probably a bunch of young jocks who ride straight up the sides of buildings for practice," I answered, imagining their youthful exuberance and young, trained muscles. "How can we keep up with them?"

"We're just going to have to train harder," observed Ted, whose engineering mind geared up for the challenge. Out came the stopwatch so he could increase his cadence to ninety revolutions a minute. Ted timed his daily bike ride to work, until he honed the three-mile trip down to fourteen minutes. With his business suit, briefcase-carrying backpack, and orange helmet, he presented an intriguing image to fellow commuters.

I usually rode with Ted in the morning and circled back home for a brisk start of my day of writing and teaching. I taught journalism two days a week at the community college. The rest of the time I worked on a revision of a book on Christian women and how they faced crises. I didn't realize, however, that I was practicing for a crisis of my own.

Compared with the women I was writing about, my life changes up till now had been subtle and undramatic. In many ways I felt untested. Could I put my trust in God as the women in my book had done when they found adversity? I believed that I would. In the few times when I had feared a serious illness, or faced problems with our children, I found God's love sustaining me.

Now I was asking God for the physical strength and mental discipline to prepare for our bicycle trip. On weekends Ted and I tackled mountain passes near our home and clicked off fifty to seventy-five miles to accelerate heartbeats, expand lungs, and soak our helmets with sweat. We were determined not to be left behind on this trip. We didn't want to be a drag, a brake, or any kind of impediment to the young, rugged athletes we would be biking with all summer.

Now at Lincoln City, Oregon, on the western edge of our trans-American trip, we could see that about half of the group did not fit that description. As we were being assigned our bicycles for the trip, Ted struck up a conversation with Chip and Ed, two twenty-year-olds from Philadelphia. Chip had toured by bike before. But Ed, who reminded us of our son with his dark hair and moustache, didn't even own a bicycle.

"I play street hockey," Ed appeared strong and confident as he tried out one of the new twelve-speed Takaras that Out-Spokin' was supplying us, but I wondered if hockey playing was good preparation for bike riding. I was also hearing other unusual ways our fellow bikers had trained for the trip. Michelle, a shapely blonde from Indiana, said she had been too busy helping her parents on their farm to do more than two short bike rides for practice. I overheard Junior, our 250-pounder, say that he didn't bike much, but played center on the football team at North Liberty High. As he tried on the helmets, also supplied by Out-Spokin', I could picture him crashing through the line.

"I'm on the swim team," said Barbie, a young-looking sixteen-year-old from Watertown, New York. "I swim more than I bike." She was tiny and seemed to have plenty of energy.

About half of the group looked like strong runners, or all-around athletes, with muscles and pizazz. Especially Helen, our twenty-two-year-old coordinator. Dressed in sweatpants and a bright orange windbreaker, she had the trim body of a jogger and a biker.

"Tomorrow morning," she announced as the group assembled together, "we'll dip the back wheels of our bikes in the Pacific

Ocean before we start, and the front wheels in the Atlantic at the finish line." I liked the symbolism of the baptism of our bikes and felt drawn to our bubbly leader.

"But you're going to have to pick up and carry the bikes over the sand," added the group's mechanic, who looked like a surfer with his blond, Prince Valiant haircut. "I don't want sand in those chains before you even start riding."

Feeling intimidated by Conrad, our young "boss of the bikes," I wondered what the other two members of the staff would be like — Doug, the devotional leader, and Peg, the cook. I also wondered what the food would be like. Chip, who bicycled on a short Out-Spokin' trip last year, had said, "The food was okay. It was camp food."

Ted and I had told the staff on our application form that we followed the low-fat, no-salt, no-sugar Pritikin diet, preferring natural grains, fresh fruits and vegetables, and no red meat or eggs. During the last year, this regimen had eased Ted's allergies and my cholesterol count. We hoped for some help in staying with it.

Peg, a deeply suntanned blonde with a bright smile and perky sense of humor, was preparing our first meal out of the two-burner-and-grill mobile kitchen. I could see shelves in the trailer filled with pots and pans and institutional-sized cans of mashed potatoes and applesauce. Peg had set up a table on the parking lot facing the ocean. Several bikers who had ridden out from Indiana in the van were opening cans and setting out food.

There was a closeness among this small group who had been together on the road. The rest of us exhibited a "new-kid-on-the-block" awkwardness. I felt like a first-day freshman at my big-city high school. Ted and I knew one other person, Barbara Haya, who was also from Los Angeles. She was the third Barbara in the group. We three had bicycled together once before, on a bike-club seventy-mile weekend trip.

"I'm transferring to Boston University next fall and this trip with Out-Spokin' seems a good way to get there," explained the twenty-five-year-old nursing student. Her straight black hair accented a dazzling smile and hazel, almond-shaped eyes; freckles across her nose added the Southern California touch. We were pedaling together down Sepulveda Boulevard in West Los Angeles. "I just learned to ride two years ago," she added. "I still don't feel too confident about taking my hands off the handlebars."

"What about shifting gears?"

"Oh, I don't bother." Barbara shook her long hair back over her shoulder. "I figure I can build up more strength in my legs by pedaling up hills in high gear."

She has a lot to learn, I thought.

Ted and I unpacked our plastic divided plates, soup bowls, and camping "silver," and stood in chow line with the rest of the bikers. Besides the variety of physical types we had noticed before, we now saw diversity in tableware as well, from Barbara Haya's GI mess kit to Junior's large plastic compartmentalized tray, almost fifteen inches square.

But he wouldn't be needing all those sections for tonight's meal of canned chicken noodle soup and peanut butter and jelly sandwiches on white bread. Ted and I couldn't believe it: salty soup, fat-rich peanut butter, sugar-high jelly, and bread drained of nutrition and flavor. We had expected something better, at least for the first dinner of the trip. Is this what Chip meant when he had said "camp food"?

We were worried how we could sustain ourselves for the next seven-and-a-half weeks. Ted and I scanned the beach; there were many beach cottages but no restaurants or stores. And we didn't have any transportation to help us look further afield. One of the group rules was that the bikes, property of Out-Spokin', could be used only when the group rode together.

I tried to hide my disappointment about the dinner; I didn't want to be a whiner or complainer. Ted wasn't quite so reticent. "Do you have any sandwiches on whole wheat?" he asked Peg.

"No, I'm sorry." Peg's eyes were wide in astonishment at his question. Other bikers looked at Ted, too. They all love white bread, I thought. I felt as out of place as if I had been with our son's motorcycle-racing friends.

In the growing gloom of that Pacific nightfall, we bikers perched on parking bumpers and the railroad-tie edging of the beach-lot to eat and talk. I met one of the two Marvs in our group. "When we pick clusters tomorrow," suggested Marv Esch of Michigan, "why don't we have the three Barbaras and two Marvs together?"

Helen had told us that bikers who knew each other would be encouraged to ride in different clusters. "I guess we know each other," Ted had said, and then added with a laugh, "in a biblical sense."

Now I looked at Marv, a muscular, young college student with corn-yellow hair, rimless glasses, and a big smile. "That kind of cluster is okay with me," I said, happy to be included as part of the gang. After all, in grade school, I had always been the last one chosen for softball teams. I was suddenly aware how out of place I must appear in my wedgie shoes with rope ties around ankles, and brown seersucker dress — my obligatory dress-up outfit. I had been judging everyone else by appearance; now I couldn't wait to change into my sweatsuit.

After supper I took my bag up the wooden steps leading to Hershey House, a large cottage whose owners allowed Out-Spokin' to use it for "launching." On any other trip I would have been examining the ocean views from each landing of the stair-case, even taking time to identify birds at the water's edge. Lincoln City, Oregon, I sensed, had beach-city charm and a quiet simplic-ity amidst sand, sea, and salty breeze.

So as we gathered in the living room for our orientation meeting, I took time to look out the picture window at the gray seascape beyond. Although the demarcation between sky and sea was gone, I could still hear muffled waves rolling onto the beach. I knew all that scenic beauty was there, and I would see more tomorrow. I felt an anticipation, a hushed lull, an expectation.

Doug, our staff devotional leader, was playing his guitar and leading us in a few songs, all new to me. Already sporting a luxuriant brown moustache, Doug was also growing a beard for the trip. He was an enthusiastic cyclist and the only member of the entourage who had pedaled coast to coast before. He had made the trip last year as one of the bikers.

Now he was staff, asking us to write down our fears and expecta-tions for the trip. I wrote, "I'm afraid I won't get enough to eat."

To look at my tall, skinny frame, no one would suspect that food was such a passion. But I ate well and often, and couldn't put on weight even when I wanted to. In dieting conversations with those struggling to take off pounds, I tended to withdraw. They considered my metabolism unfair and nearly always concluded I was cheating.

When Doug asked who would like to share their notes, I didn't want to read my fears about food, so I chose another fear. "I hope Ted and I will be considered individuals," I said, "and not just the old folks."

I also offered to go by the nickname of Babs because of the confusion with three Barbaras. "Better than being called 'Old Barb,'" I added. But the fact was that I had always wanted to be Babs. As a newlywed with a new job, I had decided to be Babs Johnson because I liked the way it sounded. To me, *Babs* represented a sophistication I had never had. What I didn't know then was that my boss, an interior decorator with a penchant for great formality, chose to call me Mrs. Johnson. Now was my chance to be Babs, the biker, a fun person, a good sport.

As Helen explained Out-Spokin' rules and regulations — stay with your cluster, no alcohol, drugs, or tobacco, devotional gatherings every evening — I studied my fellow bikers some more. Ed was wearing a tee-shirt that said Joe's Beer. "They sponsor our hockey team," he explained.

"My mother said we shouldn't bring those shirts," Chip laughed, his white-blond eyebrows contrasting sharply with pink, sunburned skin, "but we did anyway."

Junior, occupying an easy chair on my left, grimaced when anyone mentioned pedaling up mountains or riding additional mileage. "If the group decides to go the extra thirty miles to see Old Faithful in Yellowstone," Helen explained, "then we all go together — everyone."

I certainly wanted to see Old Faithful on my first visit to Yellowstone. After a few more songs — I knew "Lord of the Dance" — and some popcorn to munch on, we turned in for an early first-day start.

"The women will sleep up here," Helen announced. "The women, downstairs."

On the porch were our duffles, a diverse pile of corduroy, khaki, and canvas. Ted and I had our sleeping bags together in a khaki zippered cover. "Good night," Ted said with a wry smile as he hoisted his bag up onto his shoulder.

I kissed him lightly on the lips. As he turned away, I joined the women in the rooms on the lower level. After finding a place on the floor for my sleeping bag, I snuggled down into it, feeling lonely and abandoned. What kind of a trip was this going to be? How did we get into this anyway?

child, my Catholic mother and anti-Catholic father tried a series of compromises on my brother and me that led us from Unitarian to Congregational churches, with side trips into Presbyterian and Methodist youth groups, as well as a week at Christian Endeavor youth camp.

Ted had been brought up in the Lutheran church; all his family were members; most of the residents in his hometown were Lutherans; and he went to Luther College in Iowa, where students attended compulsory chapel every day. (He complained about the *compulsory* aspect.) I had happily joined the Lutheran church shortly after our marriage twenty-eight years ago because I didn't want our family to be divided spiritually. Over the years I have acted out my faith in Christ in various ways. Although I believe my role is to be a servant to others, I don't find that easy to do. But fellowship, such as we experience each week at Holy Shepherd Lutheran, helps me to keep trying.

As Ted opened the church bulletin to read the week's announcements, I studied his profile, distinguished with clipped gray beard and moustache. I heard his "Harumph" and knew the subject of the bike trip was closed. Why did I want to go on this trip so much, and he didn't?

I recalled how Ted was usually grateful after I convinced him to go somewhere. Especially when the trip turned out well, as our family trip to Europe had almost ten years earlier. But why was I always promoting these things? It wasn't that I was bored with my life. I refused to be bored. But I could see a paradox in that I was happy, but maybe a little worried about being happy, if that makes any sense. Some people call me ambitious because of my many activities, but I think of it more as curiosity about finding my place in the world. Others say I am idealistic and are surprised I haven't outgrown it yet.

I wanted some distance now to sort things out in relation to the world and my Christian faith. Was going to church every week just a habit? Or, was I really worshiping my Lord, living out His teachings, and praising Him with my life? Did I love my neighbor, and my enemy? Could I turn the other cheek? The bicycle trip represented a challenge to me to experience a new dimension of God's presence "on the road."

As I biked through the beauty of our country, I would not only be praising God's creation, but calling for His help on the uphills of the trip. God would travel with me over the mountain passes and also on the rocky roads of relationships. After all, this strenuous mode of travel might cause tensions between Ted and me, and with our new biking friends.

I would also be sorting out relationships with our extended family — our two daughters away from home, our son who would be taking care of our house in Chatsworth, California, and my eighty-five-year-old mother in St. Louis. As mileage across the states mounted, I hoped to gain new insights and understanding.

By digging back into my days at Mark Twain Grade School, I began to find more reasons for my insistence on biking from sea to sea. In class I had been fascinated by maps with areas marked "Unexplored." I had wondered how anyone could let a single day go by without seeing what was there. The islands, peninsulas, and various blue shapes representing seas and lakes intrigued me, too. In the past twenty years I had visited some of those shapes on the map — Baja California, Alaska, and four countries in Europe. But I wanted more.

I found a thrill in planning a route, even if it was only a bike trip to Pasadena. To plot it out on the road map and then actually cover that ground was fun for me. The trans-American bicycle trip, I fantasized, would take me over the map's mountains, rivers, and state lines.

I read *The Wonderful Ride* by George Loher, who crossed the country in 1895. He biked across without a map and, in some cases, without roads. He cycled on railroad rights-of-way. I knew I wanted roads, maps, and also a support vehicle to carry sleeping bag and clothes. I was willing to try cycling over the Rocky Mountains, but not with heavy gear strapped to my bike.

Perhaps I could find a congenial group to form my own touring party. I placed ads in newsletters of several bike clubs, such as the League of American Wheelmen and Bikecentennial: "Wanted: 12 people, 35 to 60 years old, to bike about 50 miles a day across U.S. next summer. Also need support vehicle."

Answers to my ads arrived from Virginia, Florida, Ohio, California, and everywhere in between. I was elated with all the mail, but the ideas the bikers had on how they wanted to cross America were as diverse as their hometowns.

Some wanted to go east to west; others claimed the prevailing winds made west-to-east preferable. Several bikers suggested staying in motels and eating in restaurants; most wanted to camp and cook along the way. A few of the bikers agreed with my idea of a "sag wagon" for carrying gear, but one cyclist called such support cheating. "Forming a cohesive group out of these people," I told Ted, "would be more difficult than pedaling over the Big Horn Mountains in Wyoming."

Continuing my search, I checked a list of bicycle touring groups in a magazine, and I was encouraged to find one, Out-Spokin' of Elkhart, Indiana, that seemed to meet all my requirements. The cost of the trip was also reasonable at $715. I wrote to Out-Spokin', an organization sponsored by Mennonite Board of Missions.

Now, what did I know about Mennonites? At first I imagined people with big black hats and bushy beards, riding bicycles. I chuckled at the incongruity. But I knew that image was out-of-date. I remembered meeting two Mennonite women the year before at a writer's conference; they had dressed in modern clothes. Their faith was an integral part of their lives, the leading motivation for decisions and attitudes. Much more so than mine, and I admired them for it.

I began to learn more about the Mennonites. Descended from Anabaptists, who practice adult baptism, they are named after Menno Simons, their sixteenth-century leader. The Amish sect, so often seen in rural Pennsylvania, is an offshoot, and similar to Old Colony Mennonites who keep the "old ways." Big hats and bushy beards, perhaps. At any rate, the Mennonites' belief in peace, non-violence, and justice appealed to me. I felt I would be at home with them.

But not all the bikers would be Mennonites; the brochure said that sixteen different denominations were represented last year. At first we might have communication problems, I thought; we would all use different Christian jargon. But I believed we would find a common ground in Christ's teachings on love, faith, and hope. Bicycling together could bring our individual spiritual journeys into accord.

As for our physical journey, or route, that sounded inviting to me, also, as I revived my map-reading dreams. Starting at Lincoln City, Oregon, we would follow the Columbia River; roll over the Rockies to dip down into Yellowstone; cross through the South Dakota Badlands, Midwestern prairies, and then enjoy a rest day on Mackinac Island in Michigan. That would be followed by a jaunt through Ontario, Canada, and a stopover at Niagara Falls.

Our daily average would be eighty miles, but on seven days we would push ourselves to bike over one hundred. The easiest day was a thirty-seven-mile allotment for July 8 to climb Bald Mountain in the Big Horn Range of the Rockies. Our finale would be a three-New-England-states-in-one-day run for Hampton Beach, New Hampshire, for a total of 3892.2 miles. I was excited just reading about the trip.

I learned that the Out-Spokin' name is a play on the words for bicycle spokes and on our speaking out to people along the way about our faith. A group like this, I thought, will be supportive of my spiritual odyssey. I signed up — alone — without Ted because he said he couldn't go. I felt defiant, almost like a kid running away from home. I remembered how I had felt several years before when I had gone away for the first time alone. I still remembered driving to that motel just a few miles from home on a Friday night. I considered my attendance at the weekend church seminar a daring departure from my suburban housewifely existence.

But Ted had gotten used to my stubborn independence. "You've really done it after all," he said when I registered with Out-Spokin'.

There was a possibility of unexpected adventure on the trip when Mount St. Helens erupted. Located only forty miles from our trip's Columbia River route, the volcano spewed heavy layers of ash eastward along our path all the way to Missoula, Montana. The volcano's second blast met an uncharacteristic westerly wind to distribute gray dust westward toward Lincoln City, Oregon. I was crushed. It looked as though the first ten days of my trip would be through volcanic fallout.

"Maybe you shouldn't go," Ted suggested as he read accounts of devastation, Portland's airport closed because of low visibility, and area residents who had to remain indoors or wear masks. Newspapers described the cities looking as though they were ghost towns.

I hated to think of the scenic Northwest's trees, flowers, and berries all covered with gray silt, and me wearing a gas mask. "But I have to go," I answered, secretly curious to see the volcanic dust for myself.

My doctor advised that I take some surgical masks. He said that inhaling the glass-like dust during heavy exertion of bicycle riding would cause silt to become imbedded in my lungs permanently. So I packed a box of surgical masks, along with more-usual gear such as a rain poncho, long-sleeved cotton shirts, and chamois-lined biking shorts.

I still hadn't given up hope that Ted would go. I read to him from Out-Spokin' literature that came in the mail. "I need you to nudge," I pleaded. "Listen to this description: 'One of the most dynamic experiences of a person's life.... The fresh air, clear sky, and colorful sunset help us to relax our muscles at the end of the day.... A carry-in dinner provided by church friends means plenty of home cooking and freshly baked pie for dessert.'"

Ted wrote to Out-Spokin' Director Don Rittenhouse, asking if he could join the group for a few weeks, either at the beginning or the end. I was hopeful, but Don insisted that everyone make the entire trip. An important sense of community is lost, he wrote, if some

**The author and her husband, Ted.**

members leave early or others join along the way. The Christian community experience was top priority with Out-Spokin', expressed in its slogan: "*You count more than getting there*,"

With three weeks of vacation from the year before and three weeks due on July 1, Ted began to see possibilities to join me on the entire trip. His main solar project, a "power tower" in west Texas, was ending the middle of June. When his boss advanced some vacation allotment from two years in the future to make the required eight weeks, Ted signed up for the entire trip, sea to sea. And I was content at last; I would have my favorite traveling companion pedaling beside me. "That's it," he said, "but I'd rather be sailing." I could just picture that bumper sticker on his bike.

"That's it," he repeated, excited in spite of himself. "I'm in hock on my future vacations, so this had better be good. Remember, I'm only doing it so I can be with you." And then, the first night of the trip, we were on separate floors of the Lincoln City, Oregon, beach cottage.

# 3

# A Community Is Born

"IF TED AND I can't bike together," I said to Helen as she stepped out of the shower at 5:30 the next morning, "can't we at least sleep together?" I felt as though Ted and I were under house-arrest with this forced separation. Had I persuaded Ted to go on this trip, glorified it as a renewal for the two of us, only to find out we would hardly see each other?

"Sure, you can sleep together." Helen laughed as she dressed and towel-dried her short, curly hair. "We'll arrange it from now on."

I went quickly to find Ted. He was on the wooden stairs of the cottage, peering through the morning mist at the bikes below. "On special nights," he said when I told him the news, "we can always rent a motel room."

"I don't know how it will work out, or where we will be sleeping," I added, "but I trust Helen to arrange something."

Later that morning Daniel, a biker from Virginia who had hitchhiked across the country to our Oregon starting place, offered us his two-person tent. "You can borrow it," the tall, bearded young man said. "I'm going to bunk with some of the guys in the larger tents."

The group would be camping about half of the time; the other nights we would sleep in schools, community centers, homes, and churches. Our first night would be in a church in Tigard, Oregon.

But now it was morning with twenty-nine excited people eating a quick meal of cereal, applesauce and toast — plastic, spongy white bread; washing dishes; putting belongings back into bags and duffels; loading them into the van; and getting ready for cluster choosing.

The two-Marys-three-Barbaras cluster had been scotched because women bikers were too scarce to squander three in one riding group of five. The ratio of men to women was three to two.

"We want each cluster to be balanced," explained Helen, as she juggled experienced and inexperienced riders, strong and weak, male and female, old and young. Not counting Ted and me, the twenty-six- and twenty-five-year-olds were "old." We stood in five lines as the staff moved us around like pawns in a chess game. I ended up with little Barbie from New York State and three eighteen-year-old guys, all from Indiana — Sherm, Mike and Dave, whose nickname was Junior.

Oh, no, I groaned to myself, I'm with Junior. I dreaded crossing the country with that overweight guy even though I felt guilty about my bias. I was prejudiced against stout people because I had always been skinny. I knew that many overweight people couldn't help themselves, any more than I could help being thin. But no one in my family had trouble with their weight, and I tended to be unsympathetic to this particular "handicap" or "disability." Oh, I felt sorry about their problem, but I didn't want to associate with them.

It was an un-Christian attitude. Why couldn't I love my neighbor, even if that neighbor was overweight? Did I love all mankind except those that tipped the scales at ten, twenty or fifty pounds too much? Where would I draw the line? I recognized it was a ridiculous prejudice, similar to racism, and other forms of bigotry that keep us from seeing each other as God sees us.

What if I should get fat someday, or if Ted should put on weight? How would that change my views? At any rate, I was now going to have to accept traveling cross-country with Junior. He was going to be part of my family for nearly four thousand miles, from here to Hampton Beach.

"These are your clusters," Helen announced when everyone was placed. "Forever and ever. Amen."

Staff member Doug, our guitar-playing, fun-loving, beard-growing devotional leader, would ride with my cluster two every other day. When he wasn't bicycling, he would drive the mechanic's motorcycle, and patrol our route for mechanical breakdowns. This would give Conrad some chances to bicycle, too. Conrad would ride with Ted's cluster four along with Michelle, the curvy little sixteen-year-old we had seen earlier. Conrad and Michelle seemed to have some interest in each other, I noticed. I decided she would look more at home in a pink angora sweater, sipping a soda in her high school hangout, than here on a cross-country bicycle trip.

As per Conrad's request, we picked up our bikes, relatively lightweight at about twenty-five pounds, and carried them toward the water's edge. I staggered across the beach as I held the precious new twelve-speed high in the air. "This bike is heavy," I groaned.

"Yeah, something's wrong here," agreed a biker behind me.

"I thought we were going to ride these things," Junior said.

"Give your bike a break," laughed another member of the group.

"Get in line for the picture." Helen was directing our ritual. Behind her stood curious beach residents, up early for jogging, and astounded by our invasion. Several family members, who were seeing their bikers off, held a barrage of cameras.

A row of twenty-nine cyclists seemed like a boring picture to me, but as the "Beginning of Our Ride," it was an important moment.

I gazed back at the ripply morning swells as the next wave took a swipe at me, and I bent over to trail one finger in the surf for an instant. Good-bye, Pacific, I thought, you have baptized our bikes. We are saying, "Look here, God, at your children. Please watch over us as we explore your world."

I smiled into each camera lens as the water gently lapped the back wheel. Click, click, click, and it was over. We could start now.

"All right."

"Wow."

"Yowzer."

"Let's go."

I joined the wild melee of bikers toting bikes, hobbling across loose sand — a milling mob of bubblehead helmets, white, eggshaped, with airholes decorating the surface like polka dots. Helen held up a box of surgical masks. "I recommend you wear these," she said. "We're going toward Portland today, and they say the dust is in the air although you can't see it. It's up to you, but I suggest you wear one."

The elastic band fit around my helmet tight enough to hold the blue plastic mask snugly over my nose and mouth. I felt that I was traveling incognito, hiding behind my mask, helmet, and sunglasses. This wasn't really me starting off on a transcontinental trip; it was all fantasy. I was an actress in a play, covered with grease paint — an imaginary character hiding behind a disguise.

The hazy dawn added to the sense of unreality. Cluster one's bikers became silhouettes against the morning sky as they left the beach, and we were next. Barbie was first in our line-up because she had the road instructions to get us to the first "break." We would gather about twenty miles from Lincoln City, with the Out-Spokin' van and all the other clusters.

Only five feet tall and sixteen years old, Barbie relished her leadership role, especially with three eighteen-year-old men in our cluster for her to boss around. I could just imagine Barbie with her friends at home in New York, telling them what to do, planning the action. All with enthusiasm, excitement, and conviction, for Barbie's voice carried authority. In the short time I'd known her — a little over twelve hours — I noticed how much she talked and laughed.

I also noticed her long, wavy blond hair, the kind that my favorite dolls used to have. Like the princess's locks in my illustrated *Grimm's Fairy Tales*. My own hair — brown and straight while I was growing up, now gray and still straight — had always been a burden to me. It was hard to do anything with, even though I tried everything.

My older brother had blond curly hair as a baby. I know, because I have seen the photos of his curls, which I used to consider an unfair distribution of gifts. Then my firstborn child had blond hair, straight, but beautiful, and blue eyes — all from Ted's Nordic ancestors. Now here was my clustermate, Barbie, with blond hair and blue eyes, but I didn't want to be her mommy on the trip. I was Babs, the biker.

Just like any project, our trip had to take that first step, or pedal, in this case. Barbie led us up the hill away from the beach. We rode single file. Junior was right behind, and that made me feel a little uneasy.

Also, the new bike seemed strange. While my well-broken-in leather seat, which I had brought with me, felt familiar, the gear-shifting levers were in a different place from those on my own bike. I leaned on the handlebars and tried the brakes. Stiff. I wasn't used to this kind of helmet either. The orange safety flag waved in front of my face. I checked the orange "tail patch" tied around my waist as I tried to orient myself.

This was the trip I had been preparing for, I thought. Today was the start of what I had trained for during the past six months. I pedaled a 100-miler for this; had bicycled every day during the past month so I'd be ready. I pedaled away from the beach, up to the main highway filled with early-morning traffic. Did those truck drivers know what important people we were — what an adventure we were beginning? I eased into the first big downhill.

In my rear-view mirror I could see Junior, all 250 pounds of him, starting to bear down on me — fast. I began pedaling as furiously as I could to stay in front, but my 120 pounds was no match for Junior and the law of gravity. I was terrified. He appeared to be much too close. Was he going to run over me, go around, or slow down? The hill was steep, and I was probably going thirty miles per hour. I could go no faster; my frantic pedaling made me bounce on the bike's seat. I lowered my helmeted head close to the handlebars, to reduce wind resistance, and waited for the impact.

"Braking, braking," Junior called out as he came within inches of my rear tire, and swerved out next to me. Luckily, there was no traffic in that lane as we reached the bottom of the hill. I wasn't going to be clobbered in the first fifteen minutes of the ride after all.

Relieved, I started up the next hill but soon wished Junior could show a little of that downhill-speed. He was "coasting" uphill and falling behind. Meanwhile, in front of me, Barbie was pouring on the steam. She was using those swim-team muscles to leap ahead of the rest of the cluster. I could see in my mirror that the rest of the gang — Sherm, Mike, and Doug were back there, way back there behind Junior.

Helen had emphasized that clusters ride together, ideally with three feet of space between bikers. Individuals were not to pass each other, but regulate cadence accordingly. Now I didn't know whether to join Barbie or stay with Junior.

He called out, "Stopping, I have a cramp in my leg." Great. I was disgusted at the delay. I didn't have much patience with bikers who couldn't keep going, but we all had to stop.

"Pull in at that turn-off," Doug called as we lifted our bikes out of the traffic flow. "I'll show you some stretching exercises for cramps."

We kicked stands down to hold the bikes upright and followed Doug's instructions. "Push against a tree trunk." He demonstrated. "Keep your heels on the ground."

The exercise was for Junior's benefit, but we all picked out a tree in a roadside area and pushed against it. Such stretching was good for biking-leg muscles, cramps or not. As drivers passed us, I wondered what they thought — six people in surgical masks trying to push a forest over.

"How does your leg feel now?" I asked Junior.

"Better." His green eyes had an even gaze as he talked to me. Although he played the clown, there was another side to Junior. But I still resisted any feeling of sympathy for him. His problems were clearly his own fault.

As a kid I was seldom sick and used to brag how I had never had a toothache, earache, or headache. A few aches and pains have now spoiled my record, but in my whole lifetime I have only taken two or three aspirin. So I find it hard to relate to those suffering from physical pain.

Doug had motioned for clusters three and four to go on by us, while Junior worked out his cramp. I waved at Ted as he pedaled by. I think it was Ted. Our helmets and masks all looked alike, so I couldn't really tell.

"You want to try it now, Junior?" Doug straddled his own bike, ready to go. He had a slight but muscular biker's build and was planning a bicycle ride from his home in Wisconsin to Colorado when this trip was over. Right now we were in the neighborhood of his alma mater, McMinnville College, where he said he had become a Christian. "Before that I hadn't even been to church since I was five years old."

Junior was ready to go again. "We still have over three thousand miles to go, haven't we?" he laughed.

"Why don't you try leading, Babs," Doug suggested. "Somebody must have put a nickel in Barbie; we'll have to restrain her a little." Barbie giggled and took a place near the end of our group.

I was first, with Junior still behind me. But at least I didn't have to worry about anyone ahead of me. I just moseyed along, trying to ride at Junior's speed.

The morning mist had lifted and everything was fresh. There was time to look at the trees along the way, farmlands alternating with orchards and forested acres. My spirits were lifted by the scenery. I couldn't see much evidence of volcanic ash, except where a farmer was driving his tractor through a field. A fine cloud of dust followed the machine, and as I pedaled closer to him, I could see he was wearing a mask just like ours.

The masks seemed to be readily accessible. At the Portland airport, we had seen them stacked by the cash registers, next to the chewing gum and cigarettes. Besides practicality, Oregon was also showing its sense of humor about the volcano. A message traced on a dusty truck, covered with volcanic ash said: "ASH-stoundingly good."

Several people in cars passing by seemed to be amused by our masks. One woman passenger took our picture. I was still wearing my mask, but as the sun burnt through the haze and the temperature rose, they became hot and steamy. At the exercise-stretching stop, several bikers had slipped their masks down around their necks.

So we rode along — some with masks, some without. Even though I was pedaling at a slow pace, I was steadily getting ahead of Junior. He was almost a good block behind me when Conrad, wearing a black leather jacket, came up beside me on the mechanic's motorcycle. Two spare bike-wheels were mounted on the back of the cycle for easy replacement of our flats. A tool kit was also strapped to the back of the motorcycle.

Conrad idled the motor and slowed down beside me.

"Are you with that group?" he asked.

I nodded.

"Well, look where they are. Stay together." He accelerated and was off before I could reply, but I was infuriated. Why was he talking like that to me, anyway? Was this a bicycle trip or a Marine boot camp? Why didn't he tell Junior to shape up, instead of me? Why hadn't Junior trained for this trip and learned how to climb hills and shift gears?

But I did as Conrad said and practically stopped until Junior and the rest caught up. Heavy traffic was passing me, ponderous log carriers and highway maintenance trucks. And then an ambulance screeched by. An accident — already? My stomach tightened in fear; I gripped my handlebars tightly at the thought of the dangers of the road and checked on the cluster behind me. Everyone was okay. But what about the other clusters? What about Ted?

About twenty miles passed before I could see the van and other bikers at a produce stand. Ted was there. He had bought some grapes and nectarines and offered them to me as I wheeled into the lot. "What a welcome sight," I said as I parked my bike in the line-up and accepted my share of his snacks. I smoothed Ted's beard with my free hand, happy to see that he was doing all right.

"You should see the strawberries," he said.

"If all our stops are like this," I said, picking through a bunch of Thompson grapes and popping them one by one into my mouth, "we can live through the white bread and jelly."

The other bikers were having a feeding frenzy and swapping comments about their morning. A lady customer wanted to know where all the bikers were going. "Hampton Beach, New Hampshire," I said somewhat incredulously. I liked bragging about our goal and was happy to share our excitement.

"You're kidding." The young woman's mouth opened so wide I could see a gold crown on a back tooth. "I'm going there next month to visit my mother."

Now I was surprised. "But we won't get there until the *next* month," I answered.

Helen was biting into a juicy nectarine. I asked her if she was as frightened as I was by the ambulance. "I held my breath," she said, "when I heard that siren. Thank God it wasn't for us."

Shortly after the break, Junior fell in the middle of the road, his bike on top. His front wheel touched my rear tire, and my whole bike wobbled. But that was nothing compared with what it did to Junior.

"Are you okay?" I called back when I saw him lying on the pavement.

"Yeah, I think so." Junior picked himself up. He had a resigned look on his face. "Just like in football. I'm always getting a cleat in the back."

So he bounded back, perhaps literally bounced as his girth hit the road, and was soon pedaling off with us again. I was really leery of riding in front of him.

In grade school, my friends and I had bicycled the paths along our neighborhood railroad tracks, and in the dump by the viaduct, along cliff edges and embankments. I still had a few scars on my legs to remind me of those spills. Now I'd rather stay on my bike, until lunchtime at least.

Resting in a roadside park following our egg-salad sandwiches, Doug introduced us to the "numbers" game from last year's cross-country tour. About fifteen of us were guessing the number, or trying *not* to guess the number because the "winner" would wash the other players' lunch dishes. Sitting in an informal circle under the trees, with our bikes lined up in a neat row next to the van, we each took a turn. Doug said the number was between 1 and 500.

"Twenty-nine," I guessed.

"Higher," Doug said.

"Sixty-four?" asked Junior.

"Lower."

"What do I have to guess between?" asked Barbara Haya. She had told me she was doing well, but I noted she even ate her lunch with the mask on. Perhaps nursing students take these things more seriously than the rest of us.

Numbers were called out above and below the winning number until the choice was between forty-one and forty-four, and it was Junior's turn again. He narrowed his eyes to stare at Doug. "I'm trying to read your mind," he said.

If Junior missed the number, Helen was next and she would have no choice. He made his decision: "Forty-two."

"You won!" Doug whooped, Helen crowed, and dirty dishes descended upon Junior. The rest of us cried in triumph; we had all been saved. Junior was the sacrificial lamb. He submerged mess kits, plastic bowls and glasses into a dishpan of lukewarm water, set out on the grass near the van. "I don't think I'll play that game again," Junior said. "Where's everyone's Christian concern for poor me?"

When we pedaled into Tigard, Oregon, that night we had gone eighty-five miles, further than some of the group had bicycled in their whole lives. We were staying at a large Assembly of God church with a steep, pitched roof and masonry walls. The church grounds were landscaped with pine trees, flowers and spacious lawns. Our cluster was the last to arrive, and exhausted bikers were already flopped out on the lawn. Cluster one was helping Peg fix dinner. Another group formed an assembly line to unload the duffels and bags and pile them on the grass. Some bikers (and Ted was among them) were sorting through this array to claim their own. Daniel, our tent-owner, was playing "Für Elise" on a piano just inside the building.

The whole atmosphere was one of confusion, but it was a welcome "home" to me. I was happy to be there. As I added my bike to the line-up, I noticed that tar was sticking to my pedal ratchits and front clusters. I hoped Conrad wouldn't see it.

Helen assigned the assembly hall to the guys for the night, and another large room for the gals. "You and Ted can take a Sunday school room if you want," she added. "There are plenty to choose from."

"Good," Ted answered. "Where are the showers?"

"No showers, but the bathrooms are large enough for taking a sponge bath."

Better than nothing, I thought. Ted and I walked through the various classrooms, furnished with low tables and tiny chairs, boxes of scissors and crayons, and blackboards. We felt like finicky guests in a deserted hotel. I was reminded of our family's stay in a Spanish hostel where we were the only guests. We had looked over the array of identical metal bunkbeds, used during the winter by military academy students, trying to decide which was best.

At the Tigard church, we finally chose a room with an outside window and enough space on the floor for our sleeping bags. A room of our own was a luxury, and I knew we would sleep well here. To celebrate our first full, satisfying day, I wrote on the blackboard: "Thank you, from two tired bikers."

"So how is your cluster?" I asked Ted as he unrolled the sleeping bags.

"There's a girl named Michelle," Ted said as he sat down on the bags and rubbed his leg muscles, "who doesn't know how to bicycle."

"Let me tell you about Junior —"

But Ted interrupted: "My knee hurts. Do you think Helen has any aspirin?"

# 4

# Christian Journeys and Jargon

"BABS, WILL YOU be one of the bikers to talk at our Sunday service?" Doug was putting on his motorcyclist helmet to ride the mechanic's cycle that day. "Just a short talk to tell us about your spiritual journey up to now."

I checked my bike tires as I thought it over. One of my purposes in taking this trip was to dig into my spiritual history, but I wasn't sure as to how much I wanted to talk about.

I told Doug I would give it a try. There was a day-and-a-half of thinking time in front of me, so I could work out my talk as I biked.

Sometimes in biking, everything is right; runners call it euphoria. I like to think of it as the "real thing," the rainbow, the payoff. That was the kind of day we were having. The tailwinds along the Columbia River as we traveled east between Oregon and Washington made the pedaling effortless. God had given me the perfect day to plan my Sunday "sermon." He had given Ted the kind of day he needed to ease the strain on his aching knee.

The fresh air of the day was welcome after yesterday's trip through downtown Portland. Volcanic dust had swirled in parking lots and in the gutters of the city streets. We all wore our masks, as did many other bikers and joggers we encountered. Now we were heading for the river gorge, closer to Mt. St. Helens, but shielded by mountains from the fallout. We put the masks away.

"This is the greatest place in the world to live," said a friendly city council member of Skamania, Washington, greeting us after we crossed the Bridge of the Gods. We stopped at Fraser's Folly

38

Cafe, where the council member was just finishing his morning coffee. He became excited as more and more bikers arrived. "I put in a call to the editor of our *Skamanian Pioneer*," he told me. "It will only take him five minutes to get here to take a picture. I hope everyone doesn't leave before that."

Doug said cluster two, last in the line-up that day, could wait another five minutes after all the others had left. "If we had only known you were coming," the Skamania promoter wailed, "we could have had a thousand people waving flags to cheer you on. That's the way people are around here."

Sherm and Mike were checking the map taped to the door, and Peg, who was driving the van today, was combing her hair. "If I'm going to have my picture taken," she laughed, "I've got to look good."

A dark Chevy pulled onto the gravel. Its driver was out, taking the case off his camera, before the rocks resettled. The editor lined the six of us against the van so the Out-Spokin' logo showed, and snapped two shots. "You'll be in the next issue," he said.

Off we went, exhilarated by Skamanian attention, even though we would probably never see the picture, and by the beautiful clear day. Warm sun and the gentle push of the wind were on my back, and the ribbon of blue river on my right. Our highway was smooth and there was little traffic.

As we traveled on, I pointed out a barge on the river to my clustermates. The river appeared to be flowing the same direction we were, because the wind made ripples upstream.

"It looks like the river is flowing east," I said.

"It is, isn't it?" Barbie asked.

"That's just the surface."

"I don't believe it," Junior said.

"The Columbia drains into the Pacific," I insisted.

"Let's look at the map at our next break," Mike suggested.

Anyway, we all kept track of the barge as it was pushed by its tug. Sometimes we plunged ahead of it; then we stopped and the barge passed us again. I was still working on my "speech" for the next day. Since today was a 103-mile day, our "Sunday" service was scheduled for Monday afternoon.

One of the other bikers to be on the program was Marv Esch. He spoke what I called "born again" language, with expressions like "The Lord led me here" and lots of "Praise the Lord's." I had nothing against these ideas; it just wasn't the way I talked. At our first Lincoln City meeting, Marv had told how the Lord had helped him get enough money together for the trip. Certain refunds and unexpected checks and part-time jobs brought him the fees in time to squeak in under the deadline.

I suppose I didn't feel secure enough in my faith to attribute my "windfalls" directly to God. I had trouble with that approach because there are times when the money doesn't arrive in time. If I counted on the Lord to provide, wouldn't a disappointment shatter my faith? Or would I say then that the Lord didn't want me to go on that trip, or undertake that project?

Could I say the Lord led me to Out-Spokin'? Could I say that He softened Ted's resistance, prompted his boss to offer next year's vacation, and put us both here? If so, where is my will? What about choice? Are we puppets directed in a heavenly, pre-ordained scenario? Would God put us all down here just to make us behave like robots? I thought we were creatures fashioned in God's image, with a marvelous brain for making decisions.

Although I might not say the Lord put me on this trip, I did feel He was with me, no matter what choice I made. I believed that nothing could separate me from His love. Not even frustrations with a giggling teenager who had to be reminded to pedal, or an overweight biker with a penchant for physical and mechanical breakdowns.

Our next unscheduled pit-stop was late in the day when Junior broke his derailleur and twisted his chain. "I don't know how it happened," he said when we all asked him about the tangled mess around the hub of his rear wheel.

We had just pedaled by a sign proclaiming: "The next sixty-six miles are without services." We didn't have to be told that; the deserted landscape said it all. Besides the barge, there was nothing; no filling stations, homes, towns, or farmlands. Only a few cars and trucks passed us all day. We were in a world of brownish-yellow hills, Columbia's blue streak of water, and the sun.

Barbie had turned bright red by noon. She was broiling her right arm and leg, which faced that blazing orb in the sky all day. Her matching tank-top and terry shorts were fashionable, but no protection from the sun. I gave Barbie some of my sun-screen lotion. She also tried some of Doug's zinc oxide, but her skin continued to bubble.

"We'll have to call you 'little red rider,'" Doug suggested.

"If only I could cover up." She looked helplessly at the relentless fireball overhead. In my bike bag I had knee warmers that I had removed earlier in the day. Ted and I made these by cutting the toes out of old socks. We found they kept our knees comfortable during cold mornings and then could be taken off, rolled up, and put out of the way when knees, and day, warmed up. I offered the knee warmers to Barbie — one for her arm and one for her leg.

We were twenty miles from our goal, Junior had a wrecked bike, and Doug was way ahead of us. All we could do was wait for his return. "There is some shade about a half-mile down the road." I pointed to a bend in the road where the embankment threw a shadow on the shoulder. We walked our bikes, joining Junior in his out-of-commission condition. Helen had said, "When *one walks, all walk*."

The guys had their shirts off now and I could see that Sherm's back was burning, but he said he wasn't worried about it. At first I had trouble telling Sherm and Mike apart, but now I was noticing differences. Sherm appeared more self-assured, but he said he hadn't always been that way.

"In junior high I was fat," he admitted, "and didn't have any friends. That was the year I read the Bible all the way through and became very close to the Lord. One of the reasons I'm on this trip is to get back to that closeness." I tried to imagine Sherm's hurts as a junior high student and remembered my own shyness at that age. I used to hide in a closet when my brother's friends came over because I didn't know what to say to them.

Mike's hair was darker and longer than Sherm's, and he was more lanky. Mike seemed indecisive as I talked with him, but I felt he had great potential. He had a warm, sensitive smile, and he also had a way with dogs that we met along the way. At our breaks, the local dog always ended up sitting by Mike.

But there were no friendly dogs to pet now, here on the side of the road between an empty highway and the river. As the others checked over Junior's bike problems, I climbed the embankment to see "our" barge, passing us again. About one-half mile up the river were locks that, I supposed, the barge would have to go through. As I waited I tried to picture myself on a map of the United States, up there in the northwest corner between Washington and Oregon, headed for Idaho and our first mountain pass.

I imagined our son, Matt, at home south of me, and daughter Nancy nearby. I looked toward Missouri, at least I thought I did, where my mother in St. Louis was considering a trip east to see us at the end of our tour. I strained my eyes farther eastward to Massachusetts where our daughter Judy and her husband were preparing for a Yugoslavian trip. They would be back in time to meet us at Hampton Beach.

It was peaceful sitting on the bank, imagining the earth as seen from a satellite, and waiting for the barge to get to the locks. I began to lose my resentment about the stop. God can use all things for good, I thought. I saw this break as a chance for quiet meditation and preparation of my talk. Barbie and Sherm were out of the sun. Junior could rest his muscles. If I had stayed with the others and tried to figure out the broken pieces of Junior's bike, I would have increased my mechanical skills, but I preferred this.

The barge kept moving closer. I tried to imagine how the huge metal gate would open. Would I hear a noise or would it be silent? The barge and tug were far enough away that I heard nothing as they pushed closer to the river's barrier. Just as the barge appeared to be crashing into the locks, the gate flipped up. I couldn't see an operator or hear the rush of water, but a loud metal click traveled to my ears across the water and land. I was thrilled to see the barge enter the lock and hear the gate slam down again. I had a feeling of accomplishment as I climbed down the embankment.

Doug had arrived to install a new derailleur, and Junior apologized for his constant need for repairs. We all knew the unspoken reason — extra strain from extra weight.

"You're way behind everyone else," Doug reminded us as we took to the road again. The slanting rays of sunset gave the "red riders" a respite from the power of the blazing sun. Tailwinds were still behind us, but the soothing smoothness of my shorts' chamois lining had disappeared. I began to suspect a blister or two forming on my bottom. Muscles and bones, as well as skin, screamed for a stay from the constant pumping.

Still, I felt satisfied with the day. I sensed a new affinity with the five of us in cluster two, a special group of people cruising along the river road. The night before at campfire devotions we had discussed what a caring Christian community would be. I had found a glimpse of that vision today.

We spotted an old battered Buick pulled to the side of the road; a pregnant young woman stood at the side, looking at a flat rear tire. Sherm was the first to arrive. "Do you need any help?" he asked. A few minutes before we had been stranded, too.

"Do you know how to change a tire?" asked the young woman. Her blonde hair was piled on top of her head with wispy, damp strands hanging limply about her flushed face.

"Sure," Mike answered as he jumped off his bike. "Do you have a spare and a jack?"

"I guess so." The woman opened the faded-blue trunk lid, but there was no spare — no jack either. A young child was sitting in the passenger's seat, I noticed. Mike and Sherm looked defeated. We all gazed up and down the arrow-straight highway, along the silent river, and saw nothing but bare mountains and setting sun. I hoped the young woman's baby wasn't due soon.

"We can call for help at the first telephone," suggested Barbie.

"There aren't any telephones until you get to The Orchards," the woman said. "That's about six miles."

"The Orchards?" asked Sherm. "That's where our campground is." Sherm had gone to the last route meeting for road instructions. We all gazed up and down the arrow-straight highway, along the silent river, and saw nothing but bare mountains and setting sun. I

The woman smiled for the first time. "There will be a brown A-frame house there with the name Hanna out front. If you tell Mr. Hanna that Vicki Turner is out here with a flat, and no spare, he'll know, and come with the truck."

We pedaled off as she joined the little girl in the car. I saw her push the button down to lock her door. To the rescue! We practically flew down the road. I forgot about tired body and blisters as we tried to beat the sun. We were "scouts", knights of old, friends to the helpless.

Doug came toward us on the motorcycle. "What has been taking you so long?" he asked. "Everyone is waiting so they can have dinner." He seemed exasperated at his wayward cluster. This was the third consecutive night that we were the last ones in. When we told him about Vicki's problem, he offered to deliver the message at the A-frame. "Just concentrate on getting to the campground," he said.

Although we felt proud of our role in the rescue, I could see a paradox. While we were caring about Vicki's dilemma, were we *not* caring about the hungry bikers waiting for our arrival? I remembered my mother talking disparagingly of "do-gooders" who neglected their own families.

Helen had told the group on our first day that table grace at lunch and dinner would wait until every biker was present — no exceptions. That was one of our gathering-together times, and now it was nearly eight o'clock. But the cycling seemed easy again, and we soon sailed into The Orchards, with its grassy lawns, weeping willows, and apple trees — a welcome contrast to the 103 barren miles of the day. "I was worried about you," Ted said as he came out to greet me.

But we were safe, Doug had delivered Vicki's message, she had probably been rescued by now, and we had dinner and showers waiting. "Hot water in the bathhouse on the hill," Ted told me. "It's for the migrant fruit-pickers."

"Great. How's your knee?"

"Still hurts."

A sound sleep in "our" tent was the best reward of the day. Five trains sped by on the trestle nearby, but I just worked the train whistles into my dreams. Morning brought us a blue sky decorated with horizontal, puffy clouds lined up along the skyline.

Row by row, just slightly overlapping each other, the procession of clouds reminded me of a theatrical three-dimensional effect with painted flats. Each scene of trees on stage, for example, peeks out from behind the other to create an illusion of a forest. Today's clouds were like that, flat after flat in a parade starting at the eastern horizon and ending above the heads of the cluster in front of us. Each flat of clouds appeared to have been sprayed with pink paint, dark at the lowest edge, fading to a delicate pastel at the top.

For most of the morning we headed toward this array of clouds, stopping in the afternoon at Oregon's Hat Rock Park, as we dipped back into that state for a few miles. We settled on the grass in a grove of trees for our service, called together by Doug and his guitar. I had a vague outline in mind for my talk. After Doug played the guitar and we sang a few songs, Marv was first to speak.

"I was thirteen when my older brother was killed. After the accident, I became afraid that I was going to hell. I figured death could happen at any time. It was for that reason that I became a Christian."

I listened to the young man and was touched. I felt that my story lacked that kind of poignancy; I hadn't had a dramatic turning point. At least I couldn't think of anything of that nature.

Marv continued: "Since then I have learned there is much more to Christianity than life after death. I live in faith each day. I'm on this trip now because of faith. The Lord helped me when I thought I didn't have enough money to go. Everything just worked out."

Dave Lapp, our John Denver look-alike, was next. Just graduated from high school in Port Allegheny, Pennsylvania, Dave said he became serious about his Christian commitment after he had two operations to remove cartilage from his knees. "I prayed my way out of despondency," the muscular young man said, "and on this trip, my knees haven't hurt yet." A smile broke out across his open face.

Mim, her nickname for Miriam, was next. Twenty-four years old and between jobs as a nurse, Mim had brown eyes and luxuriant, long brown hair. Her girl-next-door good looks were accented by laughter that wouldn't quit. "I became a Christian at a large meeting," she said, "before thousands of people, on TV, and everything. But two years later when I was seventeen, troubles came and I fell away from the church."

Everyone was listening intently. I felt my heart accelerate as I realized I was next. "Father died," Mim continued, "my sister discovered a tumor, and a little niece was diagnosed as mentally retarded." Mim's eyes narrowed to slits as she brushed her hair away from her face. "I considered suicide."

The group was silent, every eye was on Mim. Such despondency, I thought; nothing had ever brought me to such a low point. I wanted to reach out and hug her.

"Once I got over that," she smiled at her fellow bikers, "I decided I either had to go with God or go against Him. Going with God has made all the difference. Since then I've gone to college, become a nurse, and am now considering a career as a nurse and missionary."

These stories are beautiful, I thought. I've lived twice as long as they have; I should have something worthwhile to say.

"Mom says that when I was born," Mim concluded with a giggle, "I came out laughing. Now I'm back to where I can laugh again."

It was my turn. "I don't have any dramatic turning point in my life," I heard myself saying, even though I knew a negative statement was a poor beginning, "but I believe everything has pointed me toward my present walk with the Lord — or bicycle ride, as it seems to be." I could feel perspiration start to form on my forehead and upper lip as I told the group how my family had been split in their religious preferences, but I was drawn to Christianity. "I remember walking by church signs in my neighborhood when I was a child and looking at the title of the sermon posted for the next Sunday, and thinking how I'd like to hear that. I was curious about God, heaven, and the Bible, but I never asked to attend, or tried to go on my own. Somehow these churches seemed off-limits to me. Yet I was constantly drawn to learning more about God. I read all the religious articles in our copies of the *Reader's Digest.* That's where I received my first religious education.

"Another source was girlfriends who were going to confirmation class. Three of them were Lutheran and one was Presbyterian. I discreetly tried to pick up information from them, such as learning the Lord's Prayer. I didn't want to admit to anyone that I didn't know it." I told my fellow bikers there had been a popular song at the time repeating the word "Amen, Amen, Amen." My friend Carol mentioned one day how she had learned the meaning of *amen* in her confirmation class.

"I didn't come right out and ask her, although I was dying to know. In the course of the conversation, I learned that *amen* meant 'and it is so.' Here was another bit of information I could add to my collection." My heartbeat had slowed to normal and I felt more at ease now.

"I'm still learning," I told the group, "but I know now that Christ's love is always with me."

We all took Doug's music, the words of the songs, and stories of fellow bikers with us in our heads as we went back to our bikes and the beautiful Oregon clouds. I felt at peace with my role as biker and member of our group. I liked the way our orange flags and tail patches contrasted with the blue and white skies, and blue river beside us. We pedaled beneath river bluffs, watching as hundreds of swallows made a flapping, gliding umbrella overhead. I was overwhelmed with a sense of God's beauty pouring down on us, around us, through us.

When the land flattened out again, meadowlarks called to us and, in the barnyards we passed, roosters crowed. On the highway the blast of a truck's airhorn gave us a greeting. Barbie enjoyed signaling the drivers with a pulling-the-cord gesture and usually received an answering blast.

The winds had died down for a while, and in the silence I could hear the soft murmur of conversation between clustermates. I also enjoyed a whirring symphony of our wheels spinning on smooth pavement.

It was midsummer eve that night, and we camped at Wallula, Washington, where the Walla Walla River (Indian word for water) empties into the Columbia. Doug's guitar sang out again in the lingering twilight as we gathered around the campfire. Outside of our circle, two figures hesitated a few feet away. Did they want to sing, too, or were they afraid to join the group? Why should we keep these warm feelings expressed in our songs " — help me to be a little kinder — thinking less of me and more of my brother — touch someone, in love — " to ourselves? Several of us motioned them to come closer.

"We were wondering —" The man and woman, probably in their twenties, stepped into the circle of light. Their hair and clothes appeared shaggy and unkempt in the half-light. Doug stopped playing.

"Yes?" Helen stood up. "Would you like to sing with us?"

"We were wondering," the man repeated, "if you could let us have some coffee, or Cokes. The restaurant over there is closed and we haven't eaten yet."

"We don't have any coffee or Cokes," Helen said.

"Do you want some popcorn?" Dave Lapp held up one of our popcorn bowls.

"No."

Helen took them over to the trailer and offered them some cold water, peanut butter, and bread, but they refused that as they surveyed the open van filled with our belongings, and the line-up of new bicycles. They wandered off.

"Did you see how they looked over our bikes and stuff?" asked one member of our circle.

"Were they traveling by car?" asked another. "Walla Walla isn't that far away if they wanted to find a restaurant."

"If they were really hungry, they could have eaten the popcorn."

"I hated to think of them putting their hands in our popcorn bowl, anyway."

"That's terrible, but I felt the same way. I hope they leave the area."

Hiding in the shadows of the campfire, I listened to our words, our all-too-human reactions, and realized once again how easy it is to sing and talk about being a servant, and how difficult it is to actually reach out your hand and be one.

# 5

# Conquering the Mountain Pass

COUNTRY-AND-WESTERN music from the square dance filled the valley of Lolo Springs, Montana. Ted and I looked in at the square dance after a good, long, healing soak in the hot springs. We couldn't believe it possible. Were these our fellow bikers stomping to the Virginia reel? Could they be the same cyclists who struggled over Lolo Pass at noon? We had pushed pedals and ground out those Rocky Mountain elevations all day. Who would have thought that some of us would actually be "skipping to my Lou" tonight?

Ted especially! His knee had progressively screamed for attention, or rest. On our sixth night out, in a Sunday school room in a large Disciples of Christ church in Lewiston, Idaho, he had carried a dishpan of steaming, sloshing water up four flights of stairs so he could soak his sore knee.

Ted's clustermate, Michelle, complained also of sore knees, and stomach cramps. Later that evening we heard that Clare, a twenty-six-year-old from Milwaukee, was suffering from tendonitis. Barbie had a one-hundred-degree fever and swollen neck glands. "It's just allergies," she said with a laugh. "I'll call my mother to send my medicine."

"Try this." Helen handed out aspirin to Barbie and all the rest who were hurting, sniffling, or coughing. Ted took two for his knee. All these infirmities made me nervous, and the chilly dampness was not cooperating either.

"Unusual weather for this time of year," said a young woman at our lunch break in Orofino, Idaho. The town was part of a Nez Perce Indian Reservation. "It should be one hundred degrees this time of year. Instead it looks like more rain today."

She had joined several of us bikers at the city park's picnic table as we watched stormclouds slide down from nearby mountain peaks. Todd lent her his jacket as she shivered from the cold winds, and he told her he would give $50 for a hot shower. We all laughed. I noticed her gold necklace with the tiny words, *Try God*. Traveling always confirmed to me that there was a worldwide family of God — brothers and sisters along the way. "Why don't you stay at my church tonight," the young woman asked, "and get out of this storm?"

Helen said we had to make another thirty miles today to Kamiah, where we were planning to camp.

"Camp? You'll be soaked. If you can't stay here at my church, then come to my house and call all the churches in Kamiah." A father-son team, two Reverend Kellys, at Kamiah's United Pentecostal Church, said yes, we could stay there.

We thanked the young woman for the use of her house and telephone, and for her offer of lodging for that night. Helen told her that we would have to get moving quickly if we were to avoid the ominous black clouds in front of us.

We had pedaled nearly twenty-five of the thirty miles to Kamiah and were feeling more and more confident that we would beat the rain. Our luck, and some of our confidence, however, ran out when the threatening rain evolved into a gully-washing downpour for our last five miles on the road. Raincoats, ponchos, and even plastic garbage bags provided us protection, giving the group a rather rag-tag appearance. We changed riding technique, too, as we learned to pump brakes to slow down soggy tires on wet pavement. Since most of my bike-touring experience was limited to southern California, I was frightened by the rain and the increased danger. I took each curve slowly. Puddles were a series of unknowns. I moved over to avoid the spray. Puddles were a series of unknowns. How deep? Were there rocks or crevices under the water?

Huddling together under a gas-station shelter in Kamiah, population 1307, our cluster met another biker out in the deluge, Ray Haas, a part-time instructor, counselor, and graduate student at the University of Illinois, asked if he could share our Pentecostal roof for the night. With Helen's approval and the Kellys' okay, Ray was included.

The large church building was a metal, windowless quonset.

Ted and I took the pre-schooler's classroom, brightened with multi-colored carpeting squares. A low table held an old coffee can full of crayons. Three of the tiny, handmade wooden chairs had papers taped to the backs, with the names *Lydia, Julia,* and *Jesus.*

Were the signs part of a Sunday school lesson, I wondered, or were they nametags? I imagined a little Mexican-American named Jesús in the class. Or, was it a graphic illustration that Jesus is the honored guest at every gathering of His followers? I wished I could meet the teacher and her class. I thought of classes I had taught in the Congregational church when I was in high school, Presbyterian when I was in college, and Lutheran when my kids were small. The Jesus chair, I noticed, was coming apart.

In the middle of the night, after I had been lulled to sleep by the pitter-pat on the roof, I woke to a new noise — a clunkety-clunk sound coming from the direction of the little table. Without windows, the room was as black as a swamp. I reached next to me in the sleeping bag.

"Ted?"

"Yeah." The voice came from the direction of the clunkety-clunk.

"What are you doing?"

"I'm emptying the crayons."

"Why?"

"I may need the can. I don't feel well."

The path to the bathroom was along the hallway, through the wide area where nearly twenty twenty guys were stretched out in sleeping bags, and down the stairway. It was too far and treacherous for an emergency run. Although Ted didn't have to use the crayon can after all, we learned the next morning that several others were feeling queasy. The sick list was getting longer, and I was feeling vulnerable.

As we pedaled through the overcast morning, surrounding Idaho mountains looked like velvet curtains in a hundred shades of rippled green. My clothes, still damp from yesterday, gave me a steamy, laundry-room sensation as body heat increased. A lumber truck passed with an aroma of wet pine, and there was a mock-orange-blossom perfume in the air. A tropical atmosphere, I decided, and felt like a visitor to an exotic land.

Three of Idaho's panhandle mountain rivers — Clearwater,

Selway, and Lochsa — bubbled along the day's route. At times the percolating water would suddenly change into still, deep pools or large transparent sheets flowing over boulders to join more eddies and currents below, then back to bubbles. I was enthralled. The white-water rapids sounded like a washing machine to me, or was it a kettle of boiling water? A sudden roar of a ribbon waterfall on the other side of the road had me quickly turning my head to see a streamlet rushing to join the main river. I was cut off from the sound of the torrent just as abruptly as I was introduced to it, when I pedaled around the next corner.

A construction flagperson — most of them now are women — halted us on one stretch of road, along with several grain and logging trucks, and motorists. The lead truck carried a large sign on its roof proclaiming: Pilot Car, Follow Me.

When I nailed together the Jesus chair that morning — Helen had asked us to leave the place better than we found it — I reflected on the crucifixion. Now I thought of Jesus the Pilot. Who drives the official "Pilot Car" that we follow in life, and where are we all going? As a bike rider I follow my cluster leader. At home we follow community leaders, a boss, elected officials, or the minister of our church.

I found that other bikers pondered similar thoughts while pedaling. Mike said he used his biking time to work out future plans; Doug became so engrossed in reverie that he often lost track of miles and hours. Barbie sang to herself campfire songs from the night before, other camps, and other trips.

Ted was not singing that evening at the campground because his knee was aching worse than ever. He was tired and hurting. He said that the group's discussion about community harmony was a waste of time. He objected to the practice of frequent rest stops, usually at junk-food stores, and the slow pace in general. He would have preferred finishing each day's riding early so he could rest his knee. In short, he would rather be sailing.

When I accidentally bumped Ted's sore knee during the night, he muttered irritably as though I had hit it on purpose. Catching Ted's foul mood, I turned my back to him and wondered what I was doing in this tent, in this wilderness. At least I wasn't sick, but I felt sticky from the lack of a shower and didn't have the nerve to go into the cold river, as some of the others had done. A line from one of our songs ran through my head: "The good times now are gone; I'm bound for moving' on." Why did I get us into this? And tomorrow is Lolo Pass, I sighed.

Before sunrise we took down our tent, rolled up sleeping bags, stuffed clothes back into duffles, and ate a 6:00 A.M. breakfast of hot doughnuts. Peg was doing her best for us.

Ray, who had ridden with us since the Kamiah rainstorm, was going to climb the pass with cluster two. The tall, slat-thin biker said he didn't mind our slow pace. "It's a nice change," he said as we all pointed our bikes upward on the mountain road. "I tend to ride too long and too fast when I ride alone, and get skinnier and more run-down."

I noted that his cap had a cross insignia and the initials LCA. "League of Christian Athletes," he explained. Another member of God's family, I thought.

A car coming down the mountain braked when the driver saw our cluster on the road.

"Do you realize how far it is to the top?" he asked as he rolled down his window.

"Yes, we know." It was around forty miles.

"You've got a lot of courage." He shook his head, closed the window, and careened down the winding road. Courage? I wondered.

Ascending along the wild Lochsa River (*Lochsa* means rough water), I could imagine Lewis and Clark following Indian trails through the wilderness. Farther along was a red cedar grove named for Bernard de Voto, who worked with the explorers' journals. Large stands of white pine lined the road as our cluster made a stop for Junior; he had two broken spokes.

"Hey, Junior," said Conrad, who came by on the motorcycle, "what have you done now?" The mechanics were kept busy with flats and problems all day long, but Junior had the most breakdowns.

With his wheel replaced, Junior set the pace as we crept through pine-scented air warming up in a cloudless sky. We climbed past rugged peaks and canyons to meet up with the others at the bridge to Warm Springs. Here we saw many coast-to-coast bikers, including two brawny cyclists from Swarthmore College. After studying Junior's girth, Ted's gray beard, and my varicose veins, one of them finally asked, "How many of you have dropped out so far?"

"None," Mike answered, stretching fingers that were numb from gripping his handlebars since early morn.

"We're proving that anybody can do it," said Junior, sprawled on the ground, using his helmet as a pillow. I felt proud of us. Yes, we were proving anyone could do it. Wouldn't that encourage people who otherwise might never try? I could imagine cross-country regiments of fat bikers, short cyclists with soft muscles, old folks, senior citizens, non-athletic types (whatever that means) — anyone! Everyone!

Ted was on his bike, ready to get this over with, but Michelle still lay on the grass, face down. She said her stomach was hurting again. No one has dropped out yet, I thought. But with aching knees or flagging spirits, every one had considered it. I had, just the night before.

We were on the Lolo Trail, with nine more miles to the top. I could hear Junior right behind me huffing his way up the mountain. As shorter switchbacks gave us open vistas and steeper grades, he took frequent stops to "enjoy the view." Ted's group, pedaling at Michelle's pace, pumped its way past us. "I didn't know," muttered Ted as he passed me, "that a bike could remain upright while going this slow."

The snail's pace deprived us of any breeze, and high altitudes meant scorched backs and heads. Drops of perspiration fell on my knees when my sweat-soaked helmet-padding reached capacity. I thought it was raining at first. The salty brine stung my eyes when eyebrows could no longer stem the flow. Biking shoes became heat traps; shorts and shirt stuck to my body.

At the next stop, Junior shed his shirt to reveal sizzling cascades of flesh around his middle. "I have a big chest and a big belly," he admitted as he retied the tail patch. "That's why I have to tie this string right here in the middle of the two."

I didn't care how fat Junior was, I just wanted him to keep going. The bright orange piece of plastic stuck to the center of his perspiring back. Grinning with his happy-day pumpkin face, Junior emptied his water bottle over his head.

Many bikers now dedicated their precious supplies of water to keep Junior moving. Whenever he slowed down, someone aimed a couple of squirts right above the orange target on his back. Ray used up the contents of two water bottles on our "keep-Junior-going" project. Each time traffic on the narrow mountain road eased, Ray cycled next to Junior to wet down his entire back. As other clusters caught up with us and passed, Junior got more spray from them. He was grinding up the mountains with his own personal rain forest, plus a running commentary.

"You can do it. You can do it," repeated Sherm, who often rode behind Junior to coach his every gear shift.

"Just keep pedaling, Junior," repeated Barbie.

"I want to go home," Junior wailed as he rounded a curve to see a grade steeper than the one before. Home was in Indiana, and he had never seen a mountain before.

"Can you go to the next marker, that boulder, that wide spot?" Doug asked. Shirt off, Doug's back was turning into polished mahogany.

"See that bush? Can you just get there before you stop to rest?" I worried about Junior suffering from heat exhaustion, hyperventilation, or dehydration, all at the same time. I was thankful for the practice runs I had made up mountain passes near my home. Except for the heat, I was doing okay.

"Why did I come on this trip?" the exhausted rider panted, his red skin steaming.

"It was a birthday present from your mother. Remember? You asked for it."

"I was stupid," Junior gasped.

We sang "Happy Birthday" to him — his eighteenth birthday was coming up — and songs such as "Left-Right, Left-Right," and "We're on the Upward Trail." "Row, Row, Row Your Boat" became "Crank, Crank, Crank Your Bike" as we crawled up the pass in our thirty-five-inch "granny gear." For each crank of the pedal we advanced only three yards.

Almost fifty times during the last stretch before the top, we stopped every thousand feet to let Junior rest. When a short downhill temporarily interrupted our climbing, Junior balked instead of celebrating the drop in altitude: "I don't want to go down. I'll just have to make it up again."

People in cars going by waved encouragement. One woman leaned out of her car window to take a picture of Junior. Still cranking away, he posed with tongue hanging out and eyes rolling. We continued our patter.

"Think of lunch on the mountaintop."

"Rest."

"Coolness."

"You'll get a seven-mile downhill to our campground."

"And hot springs tonight."

"See that sign, Junior. That's the top. You've got it made now."

Cheering our victory, as we granny-geared into the parking lot of Lolo Pass Visitor's Center, were the other four clusters of our group along with several motorists who had passed us. "We saw the heavy-set guy going up," one said. "We didn't think he'd make it."

"We knew he would," I answered. I don't know why I was so convinced of that, but I was. It was a kind of "Never-give-up," Winston Churchill spirit. Lolo Pass was a lulu and a triumph; everyone made it. Ted forgot his sore knee and other grievances for a while. We were on top of our world.

Seven miles downhill in about fifteen minutes, and we were ready for our first rest day, an introduction to Montana, and a natural hot-springs pool.

"This is heaven," Ted said, sinking up to his chin in the steaming water.

"Makes it all worthwhile, doesn't it?" I agreed, feeling good again about the trip, and our being on it.

Others were celebrating at the vigorous square dance in the next building. Tony and Sherm said this was their first attempt at square dancing, but they were willing to give it a try. Even Clare, her tendonitis momentarily forgotten, was Virginia-reeling up a storm.

# 6

# Junior's Collision

JUNIOR was our group's court jester. He filled in the gaps, literally and figuratively, when we were sitting around with nothing particular to do. As long as the attention we gave him was jovial and benign, he didn't seem to care how ridiculous he appeared. If Michelle wanted to style his hair, for example, Junior was game for a backcombing pompadour, spit curls on his forehead, or ducktail swirls. He was a one-man show for the rest of us.

Every time he "won" the numbers game, which happened regularly, he was the center of another Junior-watching social activity. I enjoyed his craziness and tried to rationalize away my frustrations with his riding style. Actually, I thought of him as two people — no pun intended. He was the cyclist driving me crazy, pedaling me up the wall, and the life-of-the-party buffoon whom we all loved.

One of Junior's first major adventures took place in Lolo Springs Restaurant and Bar, across the road from our campground. "If anyone wants to eat at the restaurant tonight," Helen had announced the afternoon we arrived, "just tell Peg ahead of time, and it's okay."

If anyone wanted to go to the bar — well, that was obviously off-limits. In fact, some of our members shied away from the square dance that night because it was in a room adjoining the bar and pool room.

But first came dinner "out," as several of us took Helen's suggestion for a vacation from camp food. I had even put on my brown seersucker dress and wedgie shoes. Ted and I sat at a table by the window in the small restaurant, and Ed, Chip, Tony, and Junior sat nearby at another table. There were only a few other customers, one or two sitting at the counter. A sign on the wall, Ted noted, announced homemade pie and cinnamon rolls.

We ordered mountain trout for dinner although the young woman who waited on us said it was frozen, not fresh. We asked her if it was any good. "I never tried it," she laughed. "I don't like fish."

Our seven-dollar dinner included soup, half of which she spilled into the saucer, a not-quite-done baked potato, and salad. Ted had to ask our waitress three times for a fork. She told us they were all out of iced tea, but hot tea was available. None of these problems mattered; we were having fun just being in a restaurant again and watching the Saturday-night Lolo Springs festivities from our window.

A family was celebrating an anniversary with the square dance, and Out-Spokin' bikers were invited. Some of the women giving the party were in full-skirted dance costumes. The caller, looking like a Hollywood cowboy, and satin-shirted members of the band, all came by our window. Several tough-looking Montana cowboys, in tooled boots and black hats, parked their pickups in the lot and strode by. One had a gun and cartridge belt, full of bullets, draped about his middle. "Look at that, Ted."

"This must be the frontier," he answered.

When Junior's dinner was served, we couldn't believe the size of the piece of meat. Ed had the same. "How much steak did you guys get?" I called over to them.

"Twenty-four ounces," they said.

"Can you eat all that?"

"You bet."

"What did it cost?"

"Twelve dollars and fifty cents," Junior beamed.

"I guess you deserve it tonight."

The next day was our first day off from bicycling and we reveled in it. For the first time in a week-and-a-half we weren't hurrying to get on the road by seven. We relaxed.

Junior and a few other bikers, we learned as we sat about the picnic tables in the morning sun, had been up until two in the morning. "I won my pool game with Mike, the bouncer," Junior announced. "He's the one with the cartridge belt." I could just picture the scene.

"We don't play much pool back on the farm in Indiana," Junior would say.

"I'll show you how," Mike said. He fingered the bullets on his cartridge belt and adjusted the black Stetson so the brim shaded his eyes. "Let's play eight-ball."

Then, by a fluke, Mike the bouncer inadvertently sank the eight-ball and Junior won. Junior's biking friends cheered and other patrons of the bar joined in the celebration. Mike's friends razzed him.

A woman customer, from nearby Kooskia, Idaho, offered to buy one of the young men bikers a beer. "I want to learn more about Out-Spokin'," she said. "My son might join up next year."

The other Saturday-night Montana revelers gathered around to lionize the cross-country biking heros as Mike, the bouncer, sulked at the end of the bar. "You want to see what a quick draw I am?" he asked Junior.

"Sure," Junior sounded confident, but his pale face spoke another story.

"Come back here to my target-practice room." Mike led Junior and the three other bikers behind the bar to a small narrow room with targets mounted at the far end.

"Stand out of the way," Mike instructed them, "and watch this."

Bang!

The gun went off, accidentally. The bullet missed Mike's foot by inches.

I could just see Junior and his fellow bikers getting out of that target room, through the little door, around the bar, and across the road, back home to the Out-Spokin' tents, all in about one minute. Safe at last. The only problem was that it was now two in the morning, and staff knew what was going on.

How would I react under such circumstances if I were in charge of a group of young people? Here was their first real temptation after ten days of trials by biking. They weren't bad kids, just curious, daring perhaps, aching to experiment and investigate new things. The twenty-year-olds involved in this 2:00 A.M. caper had responsible jobs at home and were pretty much on their own.

Surely, these independent young men were in a separate category from the high school students, just as Ted and I felt we should have had different status. Yet the Out-Spokin' rules covered us all like a blanket.

What would I have done if I had had Helen's job? I didn't know. I was simply relieved that I was "just a biker," a member of the group. The "carousing" bikers said they were reprimanded severely by the staff and warned against future infringements. And forgiven, I hoped.

After a brunch of oatmeal with crushed pineapple topping, salad, and grapefruit juice, cleaning our bikes was next on an agenda that included swimming, soaking in the hot tub, reading, writing, and relaxing. And avoiding the bar and pool room. Our bikes had to first pass inspection by Conrad who seemed to have an inspector general's eye for dirt. In spite of his youth, he played the role of a commissar, and I felt uneasy about him. His good looks and position of authority appealed more to several of the young women bikers. One of Conrad's most loyal fans was Michelle, who reminded me of a blond Barbra Streisand.

I had tar on my wheel rims, which was almost impossible to get off. It had worked itself into tiny scratches and had to be picked out. We should have dental tools, I thought, for such fine work. I was losing my determination to take care of, and learn more about my bike. I wanted to get out of this chore.

"Ted, how would you like me to wash some of your clothes while you clean my bike?"

"Wash clothes by hand?" The promised laundry equipment at Lolo was out of order.

"Peg said she would heat water, and I could use the two tubs."

"Okay with me."

As I washed our clothes and my bike bag in the stream that ran through the meadow, a robin hopped about, keeping an eye on me. This was far better than being in a laundromat, I thought. I looked at the huge rock outcroppings nearby, the mountain pass we had descended the day before, and felt the nearness of wildlife in the woods. A moose had been sighted by cluster one as they came down Lolo Pass, and I saw a large jackrabbit cross the road in front of me.

Chipmunks abounded in the campground. As we assembled for our 6:00 P.M. Sunday service — it was Sunday again — we watched a bold chipmunk carry off a leftover marshmallow. It was the end of our day off.

Doug divided us into three groups to discuss what "Jesus Christ means to me right now." This time, I thought, the others can wrestle with their own spiritual journeys and I would enjoy hearing what they had to say. I wasn't going to plan out my response but just say whatever came to me when it was my turn. My group sat in a clearing near one of the big pine trees. The first to speak was a young biker who admitted that for him the answer to Doug's question was "nothing."

"The Bible and religion have always been thrown at me," he said in a sharp, staccato voice, "but nothing takes. I keep trying but can't see it yet. That's all my family talks about; that's all I've ever heard. I'm always surrounded by church people, but I just don't get it."

The group of eight bikers was silent. Were we supposed to comment, I wondered; to counsel, or uplift, or exhort? In religious discussions I often felt pressured for fear that my faith was being judged by the others, and found wanting. This young man had the courage to be honest, but what should we answer? Should we just silently pray for him? I thought I could understand his confusion and rebellion. After all, even the apostle Paul expressed his own doubts and despaired of things from time to time.

Since no one was adding comments, perhaps that was a sign that we were not judging each other. I hoped we were not rating our fellow travelers as super- or sub-Christians, or even non-Christians. Linda, a pretty young woman from Pennsylvania, said, "Jesus is my best friend." The conviction and commitment shone in her eyes as she told how she prayed throughout her day's activities. Molly, a fellow Californian from northern Arcata, said she was a new Christian, still learning about the Bible and her faith. Barbara Haya said she did not think of God as a personal God, and had been away from the church for the last ten years. "But I have always believed," she said, "and pray when I'm in trouble."

Chip told about the difficulties he had in being a strong Christian surrounded by friends who were not. "I know I'll never lose my faith, but when I try to talk to my friends about Christ, they don't want to listen." He frowned a little as he talked. "Being on this trip, surrounded by believers, helps me a lot."

Ruth, next in the circle, was a Mennonite. I knew that because I had talked with her many times. She was in Ted's cluster and often we both sat with her at mealtime. I wondered what Ted was telling his group. I was vaguely aware of the other two groups' buzz of conversation, interspersed with laughter, only about ten feet away from us among the trees and tents.

And what was Junior saying? He was in the third group of bikers. I knew he was a Mennonite because he often boasted, "The Mennonite women are good cooks."

"I've tried to live Jesus' way," Ruth said simply as she looked about at each of us, "but I haven't prayed aloud for years. The first day of this trip I tried praying out loud on the beach. It sounded strange, but the words just came. I usually think it sounds dumb." She laughed.

I told the group that I thought of Christ as a healer. "I believe if we ask for help we will receive it, perhaps not the way we expect, but we will be strengthened." I said I was thankful for my good health and prayed almost continuously when anything went wrong, a statement I would remember in Missoula.

When all three groups gathered together again, Peg read a note from Ray Haas, who had pedaled off with a small group of bikers that morning, heading for Missoula. I thought how much Ray had helped us in getting Junior over Lolo Pass; he was an honorary member of cluster two. "Remember me with smiles," he wrote, "for that's how I'll remember all of you. I'm certain the remainder of your journey will go very well. Romans 8:28: 'We know that in all things God works for good for those who love him.' Remember, you've got the best Pilot in the universe to guide you."

The next day we were off for Missoula, too, on sparkling clean bikes. Ted's work had passed inspection. Maybe Conrad was right, I allowed. The bicycles were clean, most of our clothes had been laundered, and even my bike bag was fresh again, and it was a good feeling. But we were back into wearing surgical masks because volcanic ash was reported to be heavy in Missoula. Bikers who had left their masks off in the Portland area had suffered from cold-like symptoms and sore throats.

However, the air in Missoula appeared to be clear, and there was little dust in the gutters or in parking lots. I slipped my mask off as I was leading my cluster through the busy downtown intersections. Each corner was decorated with large hanging baskets of petunias. I was feeling good for our 100-mile-day to Garrison, Montana.

Biking through a city requires a great deal of alertness and concentration. Besides the traffic, I was watching for wheel-trapping grates, parked motorists who suddenly opened doors, pavement that was uneven, and broken glass. Some bikers wipe off their tires after riding through a patch of glass by leaning over to rub the leather part of their riding gloves across the tire tread. But I had never felt that confident of my balance and control. However, under-confidence was not one of Junior's flaws.

He was wheeling close behind me as our group approached a bustling corner, after going through some broken glass. "Wipe off your tires, Junior," suggested Barbie, who was still giving orders to the rest of us.

Junior wasn't wearing gloves, so I don't know whether he bent over to wipe his tires or not. I do know, however, that he wasn't paying attention as we approached an intersection. The green light changed to amber and I called out, "Light changing, stopping."

Crunch! I stopped, he didn't. Junior connected for a successful tackle, making a "dog pile" of bikes and people, with me on the bottom. As I hit the pavement and crumpled from the weight of Junior plus two bikes on top, I could feel my leg bone bend or shudder. Although I had never had a broken bone, I was sure that was what had happened. I wailed to myself, the trip is over for me. How can I bike in a cast? And I only got as far as Missoula.

"I saw it all happen. I saw it all happen," cried an excited pedestrian who was trying to cross the street. The man was waving his hands around, talking to anyone who would listen. Cars stopped in all four directions. From my spot under the pile of bikes

I could see Junior's roundness, the overwrought pedestrian, and various other colored shapes and forms descending upon me. The asphalt pavement felt cool where my bare skin touched it.

"I didn't want to hurt anyone," Junior was moaning as he picked his bicycle off the pile. "Are you all right, Babs?"

My first thought was to get to the sidewalk. I had forgotten completely the rule of not moving the victim. Well, I couldn't do this, I thought, if my leg were broken. I dragged my bike to the side, but my worries continued. Would Ted keep going if I had to go home? But I didn't want to quit now. I was just getting started. I had prepared for this, planned for this, prayed for this. Now I prayed that I could continue.

On the sidewalk, surrounded by clustermates and a few curious bystanders, I took off my knee warmers which, happily, had protected my legs from scrapes. Everything looked normal. As I rolled up my shirtsleeves, I found one bleeding elbow. That was all, so far. Still shaking from the shock of the impact, I tried to find an old band-aid that I knew was in my bike bag. Everyone was asking questions: "Anybody hurt? What happened? Do you need an ambulance?"

Giving up on my search for the band-aid, I splashed water on a corner of my bandana and wiped off my elbow. Then I dabbed on some of the vaseline I carried for my lips. Junior appeared to be unhurt. No scrapes or anything. Our clustermates waved the other bikers on as they slowed down to check. The excited pedestrian went ahead and crossed the street when the signal changed again, and the other onlookers flowed along.

I was relieved but angry, too. If Junior wasn't going to pay close attention, I didn't want to ride in front of him anymore. We checked brakes and shifted gears to see if our bikes were still working, and pedaled on to lunch.

But my shin bone, just below the right knee, started hurting. Oh, God, could it be a hairline crack? I worried. I prayed. I worried. I prayed.

I remembered times in my past when I suspected injury or illness. One time as a teenager I was afraid to go to the doctor or tell my mother about my irregular periods. I was a counselor at a Salvation Army camp that year and adapted one of our little songs as a litany for my healing. Many times during each day I would sing:

*God hears your prayer in the morning,*
*God hears your prayer at noon,*
*God hears your prayer in the evening.*
*You'll get your answer soon.*

Since then I have often repeated that little prayer, though I must admit that all my answers have not come soon, and some have been "no." God has a purpose for the weak points and the infirmities in our lives. We have only to go to the apostle Paul to find a companion. In 2 Corinthians 12:9 he gathers strength from God's promise, "My grace is sufficient for thee: for my strength is made perfect in weakness." Even in a weakened shinbone.

# 7

# Ten Mosquitoes on Your Back

SANCTUARY is a good word to describe what church buildings meant to us on this trip. Asylum, refuge, immunity, safety, a sacred place, a holy of holies. Sanctuary says it all. But I never thought Ted and I would seek refuge in a Catholic confessional, of all places. The mosquitoes of Drummond, Montana, drove us to it.

The pests attacked us shortly after we had had a peaceful lunch break in a Missoula park. Not knowing what the afternoon held for us, we were sitting complacently around a table, all digesting two or three helpings of salad. Most of us had developed the habit of eating three times our normal allotment, and using up all the calories. Ed joined us to report on some graffiti appropriate to our trip that he found in the men's room. "It's from a song from The Grateful Dead," Ed laughed as he half-sang, half-recited the words: "Sometimes the lights are shining on me; other times I can barely see. Lately it occurs to me what a long, strange trip it's been."

"Barbie looks like the lights have been shining on her," Doug agreed. The "little red rider" was playing frisbee on the lawn, still glowing from sunburn.

"And Junior could barely see when he ran into me this morning," I added. I definitely was not going to ride in front of him anymore.

"It certainly is a strange trip," Ed said.

"And long," Ted agreed, rubbing his knee.

Some neighborhood children were looking at our bikes. The first comment from interested visitors usually was, "The bikes are all alike." Then they marveled at the way we lined them up in a compact row. One of the kids, a boy around ten, came over to talk to us. "I think your trip is too long," he said when he heard where we were going.

"You do?" Ruth asked. She was braiding her blond hair into two pigtails. "What would be the right length for a bike trip?"

"Oh, a couple of blocks," the little boy said.

Another child, in another town, had told us that if we got hungry later that day, there was a restaurant down the street. These young children had no comprehension of how far we were going. Their world was bound by numbers of blocks, not thousands of miles and state lines, time zones, or continental divides. They didn't know what we were talking about when we said we were going to Hampton Beach, New Hampshire. I'm not sure I always did either.

Maybe a couple of blocks was the right length for a trip. I winced as I twisted my leg, getting up from the table. As we all headed for our bikes, route meetings, or water-bottle fillings, Mike was telling the group about the tigers and elephant he had seen going the other way on the divided highway that morning.

"No one else in our cluster saw them," I teased.

Mike's open face appealed for our belief in his "mirage." "They were in circus trucks," he insisted, "and I saw them."

But no one doubted the reality of the mosquitoes. In the middle of the afternoon we pedaled into thick clouds of the insects. They welcomed the opportunity for a free ride and potential meal. "Barbie," I called out to her, "you must have ten mosquitoes on your back."

She tried to brush them off with her hand. I could feel needle-noses on my own back and tried rumpling my shirt and moving shoulder muscles. But they clung and they stung, even finding the air holes in my helmet. My entire head began to itch, but I couldn't get rid of the pests, or even scratch the bites, without taking off my helmet.

While we were struggling with the whining, biting bugs, we were pedaling down one of the best roadways of the trip. Nearly deserted, except for mosquitoes, it was a well-maintained four-lane highway. I looked out at the dry earth surrounding us and was baffled by the ironic siege of mosquitoes. Only in Ted's home state of Minnesota had I experienced mosquito bites in the afternoon.

At our rest break in Drummond, Montana, Ted asked the Dairy Queen clerk if the mosquitoes were always this bad. "Oh, this is nothing," the young woman said. "Wait until tonight."

We were standing in line, jumping, swatting, and twitching. In the blazing sun, the insects bit as much as in the shade, and there was no breeze to disturb them. How could we enjoy our rest? The bikers were buying milkshakes, ice cream, and soft drinks in desperation.

First I swept off a herd of the mosquitoes on my arm to apply some repellent. They nonchalantly resettled as soon as I had spread the ointment.

"Spray my back?" Ted asked.

The spray scored a direct hit on each mosquito. "I think they like it," I told him. "They're smiling."

"How do you protect yourself from the mosquitoes?" Ted went back to question the DQ clerk.

"We don't."

There was no hope. Helen called an impromptu meeting in the DQ parking lot to discuss our next stretch of riding, a twenty-mile section to the Garrison campground. The eighty-eight miles we had covered so far, plus oppressive afternoon heat and the attacking mosquitoes, convinced most of the riders that they had had enough. "There's no guarantee that there won't be mosquitoes in Garrison," Helen told the group. "Do you want me to check the churches here for shelter indoors?"

I marveled at her stamina. She was as uncomfortable as the rest of us but was willing to make a dozen phone calls or tramp around in the heat to find us a place. She pointed to several church steeples we could see from where we reclined on a pile of wooden pallets. Helen said she was trying to get our consensus about the problem. A few comments were thrown out by the exhausted bikers:

"Let's quit for the day."

"We're tired."

Tony, whose slogan was "I haven't worked up a sweat yet," cast a dissenting vote. "Those who are tired," he complained, "are always tired."

"They'll be tired tomorrow, too," Ted agreed.

"They're a bunch of wimps," Tony said quietly as he finished off his large milkshake. Tony was short but powerful. He could run for miles without tiring, and the Out-Spokin' pace was a stumbling-block to his free-wheeling style.

"Let's keep going," Chip was starting a three-scoop cone. "As soon as I finish this."

"If the schedule says twenty more miles, let's go," Todd said from the middle of a banana split.

"It's too early to quit," I agreed. I was the only woman on this side of the discussion. "I vote for getting out of here." Although I felt defeated by the relentless mosquitoes, I wanted to fight back by pedaling fast, and furiously to escape them.

But Helen said some of the weary bikers were neglecting safety precautions because they were too tired. "That's when accidents occur," she warned. "I think the majority want to quit for the day. Let me see what I can do about finding a church."

About five or six of us were psyched up to do the day's allotted mileage. We seemed to be forming a clique of "scorchers": Ted and I, Chip, Ed, Tony, and Todd. We always wanted to keep going. I could feel a divisiveness. "Us" against "them." Were Ted and I in with the rebels? Were we turning out to be a bad influence on the young people?

I felt frustrated. The rest of the group looked too tired to even swat a mosquito. While Helen was searching for shelter, Ted and I explored the back alleys of the neighborhood, admiring backyard vegetable gardens and vine-covered arbors. My leg didn't hurt when I walked and neither did Ted's knee, so we made a good walking team.

Old sheds in this little town had been converted into garages, still maintaining heavy, old-time wooden doors with hand-wrought hinges. Brick houses had iron-star reinforcing rods and slanty wooden doors leading into cellars. "This reminds me of Glenwood," I said, recalling Ted's hometown. When we came back to the group, we found Helen triumphant.

Father Pat Patton of St. Michael's Catholic Church, just around the corner and up the hill, would take us in. "All right," said Ed. He and Mike were the two Catholics in our group.

"Just so we're out by eight tomorrow morning," Helen said, "when he will be saying Mass."

St. Michael's, a small white frame church with bell-tower steeple, proved to be a good refuge from the dreaded mosquitoes. The men bikers would sleep in the rec-room basement, and women were directed upstairs to the carpeted sanctuary. Several of the women immediately began moving pews to the front to make room.

"Ted, we could sleep in the confessional," I said, pointing to a room off the tiny vestibule. Two cubbyholes for priest and penitent, with screen divider, plus additional "waiting" space, made the room approximately six-feet square. By placing his sleeping bag diagonally, with head or feet in one of the cubby holes, Ted's five-feet, eleven-and-a-half-inch frame might fit.

"I don't know, Babs. Do you think the priest would object?" Ted asked, as he sat in the priest's chair and I talked to him through the screen. I too felt we were trespassing. I didn't want to be disrespectful but was feeling in strong need of refuge. Out in the sanctuary, the newly arranged pews were lined up around the altar. Had any of the women bikers felt that it was sacrilegious to move things around?

We decided to brave the mosquitoes and go out to see more of the town of Drummond, population 494, and make our sleeping arrangements later. With Main Street bars fronting the railroad tracks, Drummond had a frontier look to it. Patrons seen through the open doors confirmed this impression with unshaven faces, cowboy hats, and boots. The occasional woman customer looked like a latter-day Miss Kitty. Bars in Montana, we had noticed, were often annexed to gas stations, cafes, or minimarkets. They seemed to be always open, usually serving a handful of rough-looking customers.

One bartender, at an earlier rest break, had blocked us from using the restrooms unless we bought something. Barbie, Linda, and I had looked from the shiny wooden bar to the one seedy-looking customer sitting there and considered the ironic situation.

"Do you mean from the bar, or the store?" I asked.

"Either." The bartender had a cough that seemed to emanate from his toes. The bags under his eyes matched the contour of his sagging jowls. The poor man didn't look like he would last out the day.

The three of us bought fifteen-cent postcards in the store, showed the packages to the bar "czar," and paraded into the ladies' room. Then we warned the other bikers about the rule.

The bartender loudly remarked to his lone, male customer, "I don't know why they can't use regular roadside parks."

"Because the parks are too far apart when you're traveling by bicycle." Doug had arrived on the scene. He explained more fully about our trip to the ailing bartender.

"Well, I didn't know." The man coughed for a full minute. "I can't imagine anyone bicycling that far anyway."

Ted and I found a friendly proprietor in Drummond at a western clothing store that was still open. "I stay open until 7:00 P.M. for the tourists," he said.

"Where are they?" I asked.

He shrugged. "Everyone else is probably hiding from the mosquitoes." We told him about our experiences with the mosquitoes as Ted tried on a locomotive-engineer hat. He bought the hat and asked if he could use the little calculator sitting by the register for a few minutes.

"Sure, sure."

"I'm figuring our bicycle gear ratios," he explained to the owner. Ted wanted to include gear numbers, a point of interest to biking technologists, in the group journal.

Each biker was assigned two days to "write up" in the journal. We were given the option of writing the day's entry in any style. Mike drew a cartoon showing Tony pedaling up a 100-degree grade that looked like the side of the Matterhorn; he is asking the cyclist behind him, "You see the hill yet?" I wrote a poem about our day off in Lolo Springs. Ted, our group's resident engineer and mathematician, wanted to supply the gear number, GN.

To find GN you divide the number of teeth on the front sprocket by the number of teeth on the cluster gear, and multiply that by twenty-seven. You use twenty-seven because the wheel is twenty-seven inches in diameter. That answer, GN, is multiplied by $pi$ to get the number of inches traveled by each crank of the pedal. The whole process seems complicated to me, but it is a way to know that our twelfth gear is one hundred GN. We travel approximately twenty-six feet with each revolution of the pedal. Some cyclists really enjoy knowing these things.

Ted calculated the ratios in just a few minutes and thanked the store owner. We walked back for dinner. The corner church probably appeared quite transformed to the townfolk. Tents, wet from morning dew, were spread out to dry on the front lawn and steps, plus a few swim suits and pieces of laundry. Van and trailer were parked on the side, with meal preparation and unloading activities in progress.

I noticed a neighbor lady across the street peering through the screens on her front porch. There also seemed to be an increase of automobile traffic at the corner; cars slowed down and passengers stared, but there were few people walking about where the mosquitoes could get them.

Father Patton arrived while we were eating dinner in the downstairs rec-room. I was wondering what he would think about our proposed sleeping quarters, and hoped he didn't plan to hear any confessions that evening. The energetic, elfin-faced priest was a jovial host.

"Yes," he admitted to us, "the mosquitoes are worse than usual. It's because of the rains we've been having — for almost forty days. We thought it was a biblical deluge. The Clark Fork of the Columbia River nearly flooded us out." The priest told us about the three parishes he served, programs he ran for the senior citizens in the area, and wished us well for the rest of our trip.

Montana was showing us its many facets and contradictions. Droughts and floods, mountains and flat ranch land, helpfulness from people in Drummond like Father Patton and the store owner, while some motorists had thrown firecrackers at us. Beer was poured on Barbara Haya by a Montana car passenger, who followed that by throwing the can. One woman made a face at our cluster as her car roared by; another woman cursed us for obstructing her path to a freeway on-ramp. All part of traveling, I realized, and somehow the unpleasant events just heighten the good times.

Montana had many bright spots. As we traveled across the plains, a locomotive engineer blew his whistle and waved at us where his tracks and our highway came together. In Montana, we could legally bicycle on the state's smooth freeways. The sky in Montana was big, as advertised, and usually accented with classic cumulus. And now Ted and I accepted Father Patton's sanctuary from the mosquitoes.

We moved into the confessional, placing the two chairs, small table and kneeler together in the corner. This is a good place, I thought, to pray for healing.

# 8

# When You're Down, You Go Up

STRONG feelings and resentments were welling up inside of many of us as we approached Butte, Montana, a tough and rugged mining town. I could sense a bubbling caldron of complaints and discontent around me. These gripes were descending upon Helen and the rest of the staff. I hated to add to the burden, but as I biked along I found myself composing speeches. I was trying to put my discontent into words.

I still looked at the scenery, noted local differences in people and buildings and details in each community, but another part of my brain was mulling over the social and political aspects of being in a group. What effect did group rules have on free spirits? I wanted to trade opinions, but most of all I just wanted to be heard. Along with this mental turmoil came an unexpected physical upheaval.

They couldn't open the Butte church fast enough. All I wanted to do was go to the bathroom and then lie down somewhere dark and quiet. Since lunch, my stomach had been exceedingly tender. First, the camera on my belt had been irritating, so I put it in the van. Then the little string from my tailpatch was too tight, and I loosened the pressure.

I completely lost my enthusiasm for bicycling. I could hardly repeat directions for my clustermates behind me, such as "hole right" or "car back." It was all too much effort. When my toe clip fell off the pedal because a bolt shook loose, I didn't even want to tell anyone, let alone try to fix it. Mike stashed the clip in his bike bag for me when he saw it couldn't fit in mine.

And now we were almost at the Gold Hill Lutheran Church, our

74

stop for the night. Pickup trucks screeched brakes and squealed tires at the corner where we waited for the cluster behind us. The air reeked with cooking odors from a greasy spoon restaurant nearby, but I waited stoically until we could see the cluster behind us. The church was just around the corner.

But the door was locked. I slumped to the pavement, leaned against the building, and surveyed the weedy vacant lot next door. Beyond railroad tracks, I could see a barren mountainside dotted with mining equipment. Butte seemed to be depressed and desolate. Buildings had little decoration on them; landscaping was a neglected art. But like a jewel thrown among rubble, the church had a colorful mosaic on its facade, green lawns, and shrubbery.

Someone inside was opening the door. In I went, led by an instinct that sick people have, to the nearest restroom. From there, still guided by instinct, I went directly to the Fireside Room, where comfortable couches awaited in the darkness. I took the one closest to the door. In the gloom, I saw another figure stretched out on a couch in the center of the room. It looked like Todd, on his back, with arms folded across his chest. The Fireside Room quickly became an infirmary for more of us.

When Ted's cluster arrived, he found me there in the dark. "What's the matter?"

"Lost my lunch."

"Oh, no. Poor baby. Can I get you anything?"

"Not yet."

"Who's over there?" Ted asked.

"Todd, I think. He hasn't moved."

"There are a lot of people down." Ted started listing the others. "Kirk's sick, Michelle's sick, Brian's sick, Tracy's sick — "

The healthy members of the troupe began cooking pizza for Peg's twenty-first birthday dinner in the church kitchen, right next to the Fireside Room. I tried not to hear about the olives, mushrooms, olive oil, tomatoes, and sausage, or smell the cooking vapors. Cake and ice cream would complete the birthday celebration, but it all sounded unappealing. Except for trips to that convenient women's room, I never left my couch until long after dinner.

Ted, recovered from his crayon-can scare in Kamiah, attended dinner and the meeting that followed in the church's large fellowship hall. Helen had said it would be a special time to iron out gripes. I wanted to be there. One of the things I had picked up from the group was an attitude that women riders were weak, slow, afraid of downhills, and a major impediment to good biking. I wanted to point out that these were not necessarily female traits. Maybe some women rode that way, but so did some men. I felt it was especially important to convince the sixteen-year-olds — Barbie and Michelle — that they could be strong, fast riders, too. I believed this might be the crux of the whole cluster-riding problem.

Even though I was sick, I had my speech ready, in my head: "Bicycling is a sport where size and strength are incidental. A woman may be short. She may not look athletic or have bulging muscles, but she can have comparable strength, endurance, and speed.

"When a woman is trained, and psyched to ride up a mountain, she can do it with ease and grace. If society has taught you that you can't be a strong rider, then you won't try; you won't even take a turn in leading your cluster."

I wanted to reach these young women with my soapbox spirit: "If this kind of accomplishment isn't important to you, then do it for the daughters you may have, and their daughters."

That's what I wanted to say. Feeling a little stronger, I tottered down the hallway to join the group. Ted was surprised to see me. "Do you want anything to eat or drink?" he asked. "There's still hot water."

"Maybe some tea and a crust of bread."

Helen was talking about plans for tomorrow, crossing the Continental Divide via Pipestone Pass, on to Virginia City ghost town, and then Yellowstone for the Fourth of July. "That's if everyone is well enough to bicycle tomorrow," she added.

I sipped the tea and swallowed a few crumbs. If I can keep this down, I thought, I can ride tomorrow. There was nothing more miserable than biking while feeling sick, the way I had since lunch. Not a thunderstorm, not a mosquito attack, not even pushing Junior over Lolo Pass was worse than a queasy stomach on wheels.

Helen began talking about the people who were sick, at least ten of us so far. "Pastor Jones tells me there was a forty-eight-hour flu epidemic here in Butte," she said. "Maybe we got that."

The more they discussed our malady — who had missed dinner, who was throwing up — the worse I felt. I put down the cup and fled to the bathroom as my stomach rejected the tea and toast. I avoided looking into the mirror as I washed face and hands. I probably looked a hundred years old.

Back on my couch, I couldn't hear Ted's impassioned plea for greater effort and speed. He was seconded by Chip and Tony. Everyone else remained silent, he said later, and he felt labeled as the bad guy who didn't care about his fellow bikers.

"What's the big hurry?" a young woman biker had asked him.

"Why don't we just have fun?"

"Good biking is fun," Ted had answered.

Now he said he was thinking about taking a motel room for us, or just going home. "It was a mistake for me to come," he said.

All I could do was groan. "I can't decide whether to stay or go," he continued. "If I stay, I'll have to comply."

I wanted to talk to him, tell him my strategy about influencing the group, helping them to improve. But I couldn't even lift my head. "Or I can fight for my rights if I stay," Ted mused.

I wished I had been there at the meeting to give my support to Ted's views, and to give mine, but I was down. More bikers would succumb during the night, even Peg, the birthday girl. Bathrooms were busy all night long, with lights in the hallway going off and on. I kept thinking it must be morning, when it was only 2:00 or 3:00 A.M. My stomach would not settle down. Instead of running to the crowded bathroom, I used a plastic bag that had contained ice cubes Ted had brought me earlier.

The night seemed endless. I could hear voices, people scurrying about, and learned later that they were even trying to throw up in ashtray stands, out in the hallway. The atmosphere was that of a hospital during an emergency, an air raid or bombing.

I thought of the service at Lolo Pass campground when I had talked about my good health and how I believed Christ is a healer. I had been praying to get well, but one more session with the plastic bag and I lay on the floor exhausted. This has to be the last time, I thought. No more. Please God, let me regain my strength.

If I could just rest, I would try to eat some plain yogurt tomorrow.

That should set well, I thought. I went to sleep thinking about the yogurt. When morning came, I knew I was well. I was still a bit weak, but my twelve-hour bout with the flu was over.

Helen told us she had received permission from the church's minister to stay another day so the sick bikers could rest. I asked Ted to walk to the grocery store with me. "Then I'll just eat my yogurt and rest under a tree," I said.

The sun was beaming health-giving rays and blessings on us. We asked the grocery clerk about a park. "It's just down the street and around the corner", she said, pointing vaguely in back of her. "You can't miss it."

But we did. I was feeling weaker by this time and saw a cemetery across the street. "How about that?" I asked Ted.

"You feel *that* bad?"

I was too tired to laugh. "No, I just want to rest."

Ted wanted to check a sporting goods store on the other side of town, so I told him to go on. I sank to the ground in the shade of a cedar tree, in between two very old gravestones.

As a child I had lived across the street from St. Louis's huge Belefontaine Cemeteries, and had often walked among the tombstones. I remembered one with a marble carving of a weeping angel.

On Halloween some of us kids would go to the cemetery to scare ourselves, but on nice days we just wandered through, enjoying the trees and birds, and looking for our favorite marker, the mourning angel.

I ate the yogurt, savoring each cool spoonful as it slid down my throat. My stomach seemed to be at peace with this offering, and I was thankful to feel so well again.

The sun and full stomach were making me sleepy, so I rolled over on the grass and rested my head on my folded arms. Sleep descended on me, blotting out the sound of street traffic and birds.

"Hello."

A male voice cut through the fog of my awakening senses.

"Hello."

As I slowly opened my eyes, I could see a pair of men's shoes a few inches from my head. I decided it must be Ted. "Are you back?" I gazed upward to see a middle-aged man in work clothes, puffing on a cigarette balanced in the corner of his mouth.

"Oh, I thought you were someone else." I sat up and tried to remember what town I was in. Where was my bicycle? My cluster? With reality flooding back, I told the man about our bicycling group, the flu, and the church where we were staying. "I was just taking a rest here because I couldn't find the park."

He said it was okay, that he was the gardener. He had a weathered face, deeply etched with wrinkles, and a direct gaze from pale eyes.

"The flu's been going around here all spring," he said. "Things have been bad. The miners on strike and everything. Lots of people out of work." He shifted the cigarette in his mouth and puffed on it. "Where is your group going next?"

I said we would be crossing the Continental Divide tomorrow.

"Oh, then you've got a big hill," he smiled, "a steep climb."

But before facing that big hill the next morning, we were hit by something worse, a theft: three bike bags and a water bottle were stolen off our bikes. The cycles had been cabled and locked as usual outside the church, but some of us neglected to take off our bags.

"Who would do such a thing?" Linda asked as she discovered that the large red bag fastened on the rear wheel of her bike had been stolen. Her dark eyes gave off sparks of indignation.

"Kids, probably," I said as I tried to recall what was in the little round bag that had hung from the back of my bicycle seat.

Hardest hit was Ed. "I had $300 of traveler's checks in mine," he moaned. "That was stupid of me not to bring it all inside."

Barbara Haya helped me search the weeds in the adjacent vacant lot on the chance that the bags may have been thrown aside after they were emptied. We looked around the railroad tracks and in a large trash bin in back of a neighboring store. Even worse than the loss and the inconvenience of doing without the bags was the fact that our trust had been abused. We would become more protective of our belongings, feel more suspicious of others, and be more stingy in our love for neighbor.

But what about forgiveness? We might ask God to forgive us our own trespasses, and easily accept his grace, but could we forgive the Butte thieves? If they were kids, would their parents ever find out where the new bags came from and punish them? We would probably never know.

We were moving on — up the big hill and over the pass, on our way up the Continental Divide. We had been through an unscheduled interlude, an instructive interruption in our trip, and I was anxious to pedal up Pipestone Pass. It was a new day.

# 9

# A Way Out

TED CLIMBED the Continental Divide with knee aching and frustrations accelerating, as his cluster's pace decelerated. Hearing Ted's complaints at the mountain top, I never would have believed that three days later, on the fifth of July, he would be celebrating his own kind of freedom.

Helen had lent me a replacement poncho for the one stolen with my bag, as we started up the Divide's Pipestone Pass in a light rain. We bicycled away from Butte, leaving those problems behind us, determined to make up our "lost" sick day with a daily extra twenty miles. We didn't want to forfeit any free days.

Climbing Pipestone was a different story from Lolo Pass. Cluster two was the lead cluster, and we stayed ahead, for a change. My hurting shin bone was only a memory now, and both Junior and Barbie pushed hard through the raindrops. Even after we hit the switchbacks.

"Hey, Babs, look down below." Barbie pointed from our lofty position halfway up the pass. "We can see clusters three and four down there."

"Rah, rah, rah," we cheered them on. "You can do it." The tiny bikers below looked up as they rounded the hairpin turns and cranked their way past scrubby pine trees. I could recognize Ted by his yellow shirt. Seeing me towering above him, Ted shook his head. The misting rain gave the scene a light and delicate beauty.

Eventually we were all at the top, triumphant. Out-Spokin's van was parked at the Continental Divide sign, and Helen and Peg served hot cocoa to revive us in the wet chill of 6453-foot elevation.

Most of us were feeling good after our recuperation day, but Ted was depressed. Not only was his knee hurting, but any joy that he had found in biking was being eroded. To stop in the middle of a hill-climb went against his deepest instincts. You pushed through to the top; you didn't lose that momentum. You didn't ask your body to start all over again on a steep incline where just to get started again was a major effort.

Ted had been a graduate student of physics; he understood inertia. Physicist bicyclists just don't stop on hills. But with Out-Spokin', when one stops, all stop.

"I hear there's a bike shop in West Yellowstone," Ted said. Cluster four was next to have their picture taken by the Divide sign. "I'm going to look at bikes there."

"What for?"

"We could buy our own bikes and leave the group."

Ted handed me our camera, went to stand with his cluster, and smiled as I recorded the moment. There he stood, as a member of cluster four, but I had the distinct feeling he had already deserted and had taken me with him. I felt like a traitor to my group.

Coming down the mountain on the other side of the Divide gave us a panoramic view of south-central Montana, and I tried to put out of my mind Ted's plan to leave the trip.

I didn't want to do anything as radical as that. Besides, I had strong feelings against quitting, not finishing something I had started, leaving my cluster, and letting Helen down, to say nothing about the expense of two new bicycles, panniers, tools, and spare tubes! We would have to be our own mechanics, cooks, and route planners.

All gear would be carried on our bikes, if we were on our own. What about my typewriter? Helen had given me special permission to have my portable in the van so that I could write up notes each evening. What would I do about that?

At the afternoon break Ted put his bike in back of the van, the signal to Conrad for mechanical attention. That surprised me. If Ted was planning to buy his own, why did he care about this one anymore? I listened in to his request: "Do you have any toe clips longer than the ones on my pedals now?"

Conrad was pumping up a new tire, with two more waiting to be fixed. His supply of forty replacement tires was rapidly diminishing as casings wore thin and bulged. "Yeah," Conrad answered as he expertly refitted the rear wheel in and around clusters and chain. "I have an extra pair."

I walked away from the mechanical matters. Barbara Haya and I found a grassy meadow for our fifteen-minute break. Some of our bikers liked to help or watch Conrad make his repairs, but I preferred scenery, conversation, and a granola bar.

I enjoyed a peaceful interlude. I didn't say anything to Barbara about Ted's plans. I had decided to wait and see what happened in West Yellowstone, gateway to the national park, and two days down the road.

Thunderclouds were forming the next morning, the Fourth of July, as we waited in Ennis, Montana, for the town's holiday parade. Cowboy-hatted neighbors were driving into town in Cadillacs, motor homes, and pickup trucks with big dogs in the back. We watched ranchers park their vehicles, and their kids jockey for the best viewing spots on the sidewalk. The men swaggered in and out of the town saloon.

Our Fourth of July had already started with lead cluster one singing "The Star Spangled Banner" as they pedaled out of Virginia City campground that morning. Cluster five set off some firecrackers, and Mike tied red, white, and blue socks onto his safety flag. In Ennis we continued our celebration by patronizing the town's bakery. Todd bought an entire apple pie, eating half and storing the rest in the van, and Ted shared some huge blueberry muffins with me. His knee was feeling better after the new toe clips had been installed.

"I can't believe the difference," he said, starting on the second double-size muffin. We were sitting on a split-rail fence in front of the town's barber shop. "The clips change the angle for my knee. I think I've solved the problem." He explained how he first eliminated other possibilities — cold knees, lack of exercise, height of seat — and decided the problem had to be with his foot on the pedal. His scientific method saved the day.

Two weeks of agony all because of short toe clips. I patted his knee, and he didn't even wince. "Happy Fourth of July," I said.

Ted was smiling, relaxing in the sun, enjoying his snack. With his knee better, perhaps he could put up with Out-Spokin' rules and forget about his do-it-yourself ideas.

But we all had to give up plans to watch the Ennis parade in order to cover the nearly 100 miles to West Yellowstone that day. As parade-watchers continued to roll into town, we wheeled along the deserted outgoing lane. We were also riding directly into dark clouds spread out above the Montana range.

Winds came straight at us, too, followed shortly by rain, and we were caught in a downpour — without raingear. I missed my stolen bag and poncho. After a drenching ten miles, we arrived in Cameron, the last town before a desolate seventy-mile stretch of road. Since everyone was soaked, Helen recommended we wait out the storm and dry ourselves on the porch of Cameron's general store.

Actually, the multiple-use building with market, cafe, bar, and post office encompassed the entire town. Cameron tee-shirts, sold at the store, depicted the frontier-style structure. How often can you find an entire town that fits on one tee-shirt?

The combination porch and covered wooden sidewalk was crowded. Besides the twenty-nine of us and two placid hound dogs resting by the market door, there were local people, motor-ists, and other bikers who had come in out of the rain. In the cafe, where several of us ordered hot drinks and snacks, I noticed a cyclist wearing the same Bikecentennial patch I had on my jacket. He said he was from Holland, and he looked more forlorn than any of us. "Tough day," he said as he finished his piece of apple pie.

Another biker was four weeks out from Boston, heading west to Astoria, Oregon, about another one-thousand miles. "I'll be glad to finish this trip," he said. "I spent three of the most miserable days of my life in Yellowstone. It rained all the time we were there, and one of our group was sick for a week; another guy, two days. They gave up and went home."

Would the other two Boston bikers have given up, I wondered, if they had more group support, as we did? How many of us would have gone home if we hadn't had the care of our clustermates, the shelter of Pastor Jones's church in Butte, concern of the staff, and always that last resort of riding in the van? I felt dismay again at Ted's idea to go off on our own.

When the rains finally moved on, we left Cameron to face headwinds again. Mike led the cluster; I was in second place. We met the wind with renewed vigor. We challenged the forces howling at us and pedaled toward a mountain gorge, which appeared only as a notch on the horizon. We were in the "slot," as far as the wind was concerned, going against the grain. I looked in my rear-view mirror to see how the others were doing and noticed that our cluster had quickly divided into twins and triplets. Mike and I were about a half-mile ahead of Barbie, Junior, and Sherm.

"Mike, we're getting ahead of them again." I was feeling rebellious at the stay-together rule and ready to attack the wind aggressively. "But let's not slow down yet."

"Okay," Mike was an agreeable biking companion, a strong rider. He usually suffered in silence when cluster-riding had me babbling like a crazy person. "It's harder to go through the wind that slow," I said. "We can wait up when the road bends ahead." I knew I was disobeying Out-Spokin' rules. Perhaps I was catching Ted's rebellion.

Mike and I tried to put our troubles behind us, quite literally. We were soon dropping down into the lush Madison River Valley. Our morning had shown us a world of purple sage and mesquite, and various browns in rocks and sand. Now the river valley presented incredible green grasslands and a blue, white-capped river, with the backdrop of blue-shaded mountains topped with snow. The scene, with pastures sparsely populated by cattle and horses, cried for a color photographer or a painter in oils. Surely, Ted's spirit would soar in these surroundings, and he would drop his shopping plans for the West Yellowstone cycle shop. On the other hand, he might figure that he could enjoy this kind of world better on his own.

On my right, I saw three mares posing in the scenic splendor — a palomino, bay, and shiny black beauty. Each had a matching foal at her side. "Mike, look."

"Yeah, I see them." Mike had a natural affinity with animals. In his musings about future plans, whether to go to college or not, one of his dreams was to be a veterinarian.

But we hadn't figured out the slow-pace problem yet. Mike and I eased off to allow Barbie's group to join us, so we were now making poor time against the wind. At lunchtime, Helen said, "I have a dream of getting to West Yellowstone by 5:30 tonight."

But that sounded like a nightmare instead of a dream to most of the group, tired out and defeated by the rain and wind combination. Those of us willing to continue were overruled again: Helen settled for a sixty-five-mile day; we camped at Beaver Creek, thirty miles from the Montana-Wyoming border town of West Yellowstone.

The next morning we bicycled around Lake Hebgen. The road had a quietness so profound that the only sounds were cracks of expanding metal guard-rails in the sun and a faint, droning motor of a distant fishing boat. Mornings were always an inspiration to me on this trip — a fresh beginning, another chance.

Across the lake I noticed a strange red tinge among the trees on the far mountain. The landscape reminded me of a paint-by-number picture in which the painter used the wrong number — too much red. As we approached closer to the forest surrounding the lake, we saw that the red tinge represented dead trees; killed by automobile pollutants, we were told.

In West Yellowstone we joined these multitudes of cars and tourists. Not only was there a bike shop in town, but there were also souvenir shops, grocery stores, restaurants, sporting goods stores, and clothing boutiques. Ted and I felt as though we were walking through Coney Island, Las Vegas, and Beverly Hills as we headed for the bike store. I wondered if we were heading for High Noon.

Row upon row of shiny new bikes greeted us there. On the walls were bike bags, panniers, water bottles, tool kits — everything we needed. I was breathless at the idea of buying a bike and other equipment and taking off. "How much are the bags?" Ted asked me. "How much are the bikes?" I knew his credit card was in his pocket. I read off some of the tags.

"What kind of bike would you buy?" I asked.

"The Peugeot looks like the best here."

Mike, Ed, and Chip came into the shop. Ted joked with them.

"Let's just buy bikes and take off."

"I feel like it," Chip said. He and Ed were constantly in trouble for trying to sneak a beer in their free time.

"Sounds good to me," Ed agreed. He was looking at bike bags, just as I was, to replace the things stolen in Butte. Mike was trying on bike gloves.

When I selected my new bag and poncho, I saw that Ted was still looking at bikes and bags. "I'm getting these, Ted. What are you buying?"

"Nothing."

Ted looked longingly at the bikes, but I felt an immense sense of relief for both of us. "Two days ago I would have done it in a minute," he said, "but today was actually a good day. My knee is okay and Michelle has been riding pretty well. Maybe the crisis is over."

Yellowstone dazzled us with its thermal spectacles, bubbling mud, bursts of scalding water spitting from murky depths, pools formed by steaming springs and colored by algae and bacteria; its own Grand Canyon; and spectacular Yellowstone Falls. Old Faithful would be scratched from our itinerary; biking the extra 15 miles to see the famous geyser was voted down by the group.

What is Yellowstone without Old Faithful, I wondered.

"The Great Fountain is almost as good," Helen answered, "and that is only two miles from here." We were in a parking lot surrounded by pine trees, with glimpses of meadows and mountains through the branches. Some of our bikers did not want to go any farther.

"Why can't those who want to see the Great Fountain form a cluster and go," suggested Barbara Haya, one of the tired-out sightseers. "The rest of us can wait here."

"Conrad could come along on the motorcycle, if you're worried about breakdowns." Ted tried to encourage Helen to say yes.

She reluctantly agreed: "But never again. Just this once."

How many wanted to go? Ted and I, Dave Lapp, Chip, Brian, and Sherm formed the first cluster. Ted was leading and we flew. He was unleashed and wild. I was proud to see him setting the pace for our group of hotshots. We were escaping control, we were free. We weren't riding unsafely, either, just fast. In the easy second position, I was pumping hard to keep up. I felt my body react, "Hey, what's going on?"

But after the first shock to my system, I found I could keep up the fast cadence and even feel good doing it. I was awake to every sensation: the wind on my face, my expanded lungs, the tingling of increased circulation, my pumping legs against the leather saddle, and alertness of mind. I felt like laughing or singing. We arrived at the Great Fountain, breathless and exhilarated. "This is the high point of the trip," Chip said. "We were really booking."

Carloads of tourists were leaving the site of the geyser. "You just missed it," one woman said, "and it only erupts every ten hours."

Oh, no. I looked at Ted, our inspired leader; we laughed in despair. I had a penchant for going places on the day the doors were closed. I often made special trips to stores on their annual closed-for-inventory day. I once took a whole group of women to an antique auction on the first day the place had been closed in fifty years.

An elderly man with clipboard and pencil approached our group. "The geyser isn't finished," he said quietly, "In ten minutes it will spout some more."

"Do you keep track of it?" I asked, excited at our second chance at the geyser.

"I'm retired," he said, "and have the time. I'm a volunteer park employee." He adjusted his tweed golfer's cap as the bikers gathered around him. "I've written down the geyser's times for the past five years," he said. "Official records go back 100 years."

"Then it must be true."

"Let's get our cameras all set."

"We're lucky this time."

Two more "special" clusters arrived, and Conrad on his motorcycle, so there were about fifteen of us. Our clipboard guide stayed with us as we lined up on the boardwalk. Cameras were focused and aimed at the center of the sloping, pastel-colored rock "stage." From the center vent, steam was escaping and water would soon shoot out. We heard some preliminary gurgles. I was only twenty feet away and was excited with the suspense.

"There she blows."

The water, heated deep within the earth, was boiling through fractured bedrock to put on a five-minute show for us. Streams of water rose fifty feet in the air, and pressure-cooker sounds burst from underground. Our volunteer record-keeper explained how the eruption starts when steam formed by boiling water expands to seventeen-hundred times its original volume — a tremendous, driving force.

We were seeing the Great Fountain get its second wind. I felt fulfilled. Ted was here, acclaimed for his leadership role among the young scorcher bike-riders. We were still together in our cross-country adventure, and surrounded by many of our Out-Spokin' family.

Together we had been through rains, breakdowns, accidents, illness, and weariness. I wished the entire group could see this special wonder of God's world.

# 10

# The Broken Circle

TODD WAS MISSING and nobody knew where he was. Peg and Doug had searched through the campground woods for an hour and couldn't find him. Where was he? Why did he leave? I was worried and thought back several days, to the few contacts I had had with Todd, trying to find clues as to why he would run away.

On Saturday when we camped at Yellowstone, the park ranger came by on his bicycle to tell us about the hot springs, bicycle routes in the park, and a camp program at eight that night. "Are you going to the program?" Todd had asked me.

He was helping Daniel set up the tent that the two of them shared, as Ted and I put ours nearby in the crowded grounds.

"I'd like to," I told him, "but there's so much to do tonight with the hot springs, devotions, and showers. I might not have time, and the hot springs are my top priority," Ted and I hurried off, down the path to the springs.

Todd was a loner; he had not found a buddy in the group. Only sixteen, he seemed much older in his independence and interests, philosophical ideas, and gourmet food tastes. Based on information from my previous job, writing for teachers of gifted children, I saw parallels in Todd with characteristics found in high-IQ students. He had the typical wide-ranging curiosity, a questioning mind, but unfortunately, the disdain or arrogance that some gifted people develop. He appeared to harbor an excessive amount of belligerence.

Todd and I became acquainted early in the trip because we were often together at the head of the chow line, and met again at the food table when we were filling our plates for the second or third time. The amount of food this pencil-thin teenager could eat was unbelievable, even to me. At one fifteen-minute break, he ate eleven doughnuts.

However, he was usually alone, and I felt bad about not including him in our trip to the hot springs. But I didn't have to be Mama, I kept reminding myself as I fought off my tendency to be "social director."

Ted and I reached the steamy creek by crossing a meadow next to the campgrounds. Disembodied heads seemed to float on the surface of the natural hot springs. As we approached, we could tell that some of the bobbing heads belonged to bikers Ed, Chip, Kirk, and Junior.

Ted and I quickly threw off our towels. We escaped mosquitoes and evening chill by sinking into the shallow, soothing warm water. About twenty people shared this unusual bathtub and we all watched the sunset-colored clouds moving overhead. It was ecstasy. Who could possibly have any hangups in this kind of setting?

Todd had never joined us in the creek, but he did sit next to me in the campfire circle. He was nice-looking with his thick, wavy brown hair that he combed back from his forehead.

Todd's home was South Bend, Indiana, where he had three sisters, and his father had a sales job that kept him traveling. Todd's clothes were nice, and he seemed to have more spending money than anyone else.

In our campfire circle, we were reconstructing the warm "hot springs" feelings we had just experienced. Doug suggested an "appreciation" exercise. "Tell us one thing you appreciate about the person on your left," he said. "We've been together two-and-a-half weeks and should know each other well enough to single out one special trait. We'll just go around the circle."

Ted was sitting on my left side now, which meant I would say something about him.

Conrad said he appreciated Peg's craziness, and her cooking; Peg admired Sherm's commitment to the Lord; and Sherm mentioned Linda's quietness plus her ability to say something meaningful when she spoke.

Should I say something about Ted that would make him happy,

or would it be better to point out a hidden trait, unknown to the group? Or should I say something profound, or witty, that would make me look good? And what would Todd say about me?

Linda pointed out Doug's sense of humor and sincerity in his faith; Mike appreciated Barbie's bubbly personality and the fact that she never got mad. That was true, I thought, feeling admiration for Mike's discerning comment, and Barbie's congeniality.

Checking the circle to see how soon my turn would be, I saw that Michelle was on Ted's left. What would he say about her?

It was Ruth's turn to say what she appreciated about Todd. She recalled a pleasant quiet time with Todd, apart from the group, reading over the group journal together. She said she was glad that they had shared the daily accounts that way. I was happy that someone else had played Mama or friend to Todd. He was in cluster five with Daniel, Brian, Tracy, and Barbara Haya, and they were supportive, Barbara told me later. But we were all human, too, and sometimes Todd was the butt of jokes, ridiculed for his stubbornness, and called a wimp.

Todd surprised me now by telling the group he admired my energy: "Most women her age wouldn't be doing anything more than planting a garden." We all laughed and I pictured my grandmother, when she was in her seventies, tending her vegetable garden. I felt good about the remark. I smiled at Todd and couldn't tell that Todd was hurting then.

Now it was my turn: "I've known Ted since before any of you were born, and there isn't time to mention all the things I appreciate about him. But there is one particular trait that makes me feel good. When my cluster comes in late, Ted always meets me with a snack — a piece of fruit, can of juice, or a granola bar — and I really appreciate that."

Ted's beard and moustache parted company as he smiled, and I knew he appreciated what I said.

"I like the way Michelle has improved her riding," he said. Michelle looked flustered by Ted's compliment, but pleased. After all of Ted's complaints, it was quite a tribute.

Although each of us in the appreciation circle had only spoken about one other person, I felt a sense of corporate, family sharing — a distinct aura, a spirit of love. The evening program closed with the song, "They will know we are Christians by our love." Did Todd get that message? Did he still feel separate?

My peaceful feeling of community spilled over to Sunday morning. We were on the road early, cycling past mists rising from stream valleys, fumaroles, and thermal springs, and through Yellowstone's wildlife preserves. A mother moose and baby watched us glide by from their hiding place in a glen, elk grazed in the meadows, and buffalo herds dotted the open range.

Wispy spider webs bridged the roads. They crossed my face, fluttered from Sherm's safety flag, and clung to Junior's shoulders like a gossamer neck scarf. We were saying farewell to Yellowstone Park, heading for Sylvan Pass, the park's eastern exit. There were promises of snow on the pass.

A huge snowbank — maybe thirty feet wide, plunging 100 feet down the mountainside — beckoned to the bikers at the sunny pass. We parked bikes along the road to climb the cascading rubble and rocks to reach the snow. Todd was one of the enthusiastic participants.

**Cluster four crosses the Yellowstone Bridge, with Ruth in the lead.**

"Keep your helmets on," Helen shouted as each cluster wheeled in, "if you want to slide in the snow."

Tony reached the top of the snow bank for the first run down, while the rest of us were spread out on the mountain of rocks below him. Ted and I watched from the lower edge of the snow as the colorful climbers moved up the dark mountain. Tony dug his heels into the top crust of snow as he sat on his plastic tailpatch for the slippery slide down the chute. "Look out below," he cried, picking up his heels, and barreling down the snowy descent. "Wahoo, wahoo."

"Go, Tony, go."

"How are you going to stop?"

I knew I wasn't going to try it; it looked too dangerous. Tony's powerful legs pushed against the crystallized ice near the end of the run. As he slowed, he jumped to his feet, made a circular turn, and ran safely off to one side. "That was great," he said. "I'm going to do it again."

Wearing shorts and no shirt, Chip roared down the "center lane" next, sliding off his tail patch as he gathered speed. He stopped short of the rocks at the end by throwing his weight to the side. "That's cold," he said as he brushed snow off bare back and legs.

Helen and Molly were adventurous enough to try the lower end of the snow slide, while Dave Lapp steamed down the chute, far to one side. Twisting away from the rocks, he came to a halt just in time. Junior, wearing shorts and tank top, was climbing up to the top.

"Get Junior's picture," I said to Ted. "There he goes."

But Junior slipped as he made the transition from rock to snow. Without the chance to push himself out in the direction of the center, he began catapulting down the mountain, too close to the edge of the snowbank and the menacing rubble.

"Get in the middle, Junior."

"Watch out."

"Slow down."

"Dig your heels in."

But Junior, veering in the wrong direction, seemed powerless to act. He slid right into the rocks, off the snow. A few abrupt jolts on the rock's sharp edges and he rolled to a stop.

"Oh, no."

"Junior!"

"Are you hurt?"

"No more sliding," Helen called as she quickly climbed the rocks to help him.

"Just one more." Tony had arrived again at the very crest of the snowbank.

Helen was busy trying to reach the injured. "Are you hurt, Junior?"

"Not too bad," he called from his higher perch, examining his scrapes. "It's nothing."

Tony was posed at the top. "This will be the last."

"No," Helen insisted, but down he went, like a biker on a downhill with a tailwind. He steered by shifting weight and stopped by sheer muscle power. On his feet, with a kind of skating motion in a circle, he ended upright, walking across the rocks. Junior showed us his scrapes on thigh, back, and arms when he came down to the road. Helen had cleaned the wounds and applied antiseptic. "You really barreled into those rocks," I said. "Didn't it hurt?"

"Just a little bit," he sighed. I felt sorry for him.

Our campground that night, just east of Yellowstone, was across the road from a big lodge, store, and restaurant. There was a dining deck that looked up to the mountain peaks and down at horse trails and winding mountain road. Ted and I took the evening off to have dinner there.

A horseback riding party was coming in after a day on the trail, and we watched them dismount. The trail leader tied the six horses to the rail and took the saddles off as the weary riders tottered off to their cabins. The leader, in well-worn leather chaps and battered cowboy hat, strode past us on his way to the store. A hunting dog followed at his heels.

"This is the good life," I said, relaxing enough to meld into the peaceful scene.

"It's good to get away," Ted agreed. The mountain trout was delicious, followed by homemade apple pie, so the dinner was a success. It was an escape hatch, a vacation from our vacation. We didn't know at the time that Todd needed an escape more than we did. Would everything have been different if we had invited him to join us?

I first learned that Todd had run off as four clusters waited at our first rest stop at Trail's Inn Motel and store near Cody, Wyoming. Doug arrived by motorcycle to tell us that Todd had walked off while Helen was chastising him for missing devotions the night before and not helping his cluster with the dishes. Todd just turned aside, she said, disappeared into the woods, and hadn't been seen since.

"Peg and I searched for an hour," Doug said. Usually joking, Doug was serious now. What do you do when one of the bikers you're responsible for is missing? How do you tell parents that? The staff had tremendous responsibilities, I realized.

What would Todd do? Where would he go? Would he hitchhike to get away? Did he have any money with him? He usually did. Or would he just wander in the woods and get lost? Maybe he was like the little kid who hid in the closet just long enough to scare his parents. I used to fantasize how my parents would be sorry if I disappeared. Now I was trying to find explanations to cover my panic.

And how was the rest of the group reacting to Todd's escapade? After all, he was delaying us several hours. We had arisen at 5:30 A.M. on one of the coldest mornings of the trip, to make our 101 miles to Lovell, Wyoming. Now we were halted. Who could blame us if we resented the delay?

But what if he wasn't found? What if something tragic happened? Would we feel guilty for not actively listening to Todd, taking more time to talk with him, to sit down next to him at meals and make an effort to include him in all activities? Had he been picked on more than he could handle? Had we all been insensitive to his cries for help?

Helen called us all together on the porch.

"Doug has gone back to help Peg look for Todd," she said. "We'll just have to wait now. I think Todd needed a lot more love than we realized. Why don't we all pray for him?"

Sitting on porch rails and steps, on a few wooden lawn chairs, and leaning against the rough wood of the store, twenty-six bikers bowed heads and closed eyes as Helen prayed. She asked for God's presence to take care of Todd wherever he was, and for His guidance in helping us know what to do. "We don't know where Todd is now, or what is happening to him," she prayed, "but help us all to get through this difficult time. In Jesus' name, amen." In Jesus' name, I prayed to myself.

Helen said we might be here at Trail's Inn another hour; I saw a sign for showers at $2.50 and thought I'd try it. Todd had said a few days ago, I recalled, that he would pay $50 for a hot shower.

The storekeeper gave me a towel and bar of soap and directed me to the ladies' shower building in the back of the property. After a leisurely, satisfying shower and shampoo, I dressed and then relaxed on the grass at the side of the building and dried my hair in the sun. I was trying to forget the Todd crisis; there was nothing I could do anyway.

"Pssssst. Babs."

I looked through the bushes at the side of the building and saw Ed standing there with a towel wrapped around him.

"Babs," he repeated. "They stole my clothes while I was taking a shower."

"Oh, no," I laughed. "I'll go see if I can find them."

Most of the gang were still sitting on the porch. They admitted they knew where Ed's clothes were.

"Give them to me," I pleaded.

"Never."

"The poor guy. What's he going to do?" I asked.

"That's his problem."

"Where are the clothes?" I spotted them wadded up behind the wooden chair Junior was sitting in. But Tony was standing guard. I tried to grab the clothes but was no match for "tough" Tony.

"Oh, come on, guys," I said as I stepped back.

"Let him suffer a while," Tony said.

"Just a little bit longer," Junior smiled up at me from his chair. I reported the situation back to my towel-clad friend in the bushes. "Do you have any clothes I can borrow?" Ed asked.

"Yes! My jogging suit. It'll be just the thing." It's over here in my bike bag.

Ed was taller than I, but slim. He took the pants and rushed back to the men's shower. I dashed for the porch to see what would happen. Dressed only in my bright red sweat pants, Ed appeared around the corner of the store. Heading straight for Chip, he grabbed the neck of his shirt. "Give me back my clothes."

"I don't have them." Chip's sunburned face turned even redder than usual.

"Tony did it then." Ed wheeled around, spotted the clothes, and pushed through the blockade. The game was over.

Life had gone on for us. Under the layer of business-as-usual, or fun-as-usual, was a nagging fear of the unknown, the unresolved disappearance of Todd. It was two hours before we heard the roar of Doug's motorcycle coming up the highway. We watched him approach and turn into the gravel parking lot. He turned off the motor and removed his helmet before speaking. "We found Todd," he said, "and he's safe."

That's all Doug told us. I was relieved but perplexed, scrambled up inside.

Helen added, "We can leave now."

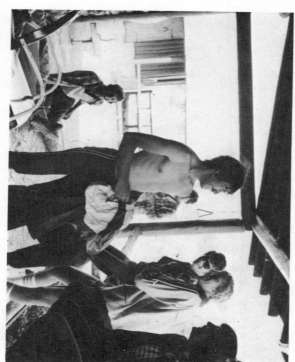

**Ed gets his clothes back.**

# 11

# Big Horn Lures Us On

THE GOOD NEWS: only 37 miles today (up the Big Horn mountain range).

The bad news: we'll be climbing 6000 feet (to sleep on Bald Mountain).

We began the big climb with Todd back with us again. Nothing official had been said about the runaway incident, although I kept expecting something. I had wondered how Helen was going to handle the situation, but I still didn't know. Should Todd know that his actions inconvenienced the group, or should we cover any resentment we might be hiding? Should we tell Todd we were glad he was back, or act as though nothing had happened?

After Doug had told us that the lost had been found, Peg had driven up in the van with Todd beside her. "We can all go now," was all that Helen had said.

Is that it? I thought. Nothing more? No explanations. Not even a "no comment." Maybe later, I thought, at devotions or a special gathering we would talk about it. Yet I still felt something was needed now. As I went to my bike, I passed Todd. He had left the van and was headed for the store. He looked unscathed, unchanged, same as usual. I experienced a sense of unreality about the situation, an absence of emotion.

"I'm glad you're okay," I said.

"Thanks."

I couldn't tell what he was thinking, but I felt better because I had said something to him. My next contact with Todd was at lunch in the city park in Cody, Wyoming.

We had just heard that the U.S. hostages in Iran had been moved from the embassy. Todd was in our group of bikers, sitting on the lawn, discussing the situation. Mim, who had had a yellow ribbon tied onto her bike bag since the beginning of the trip, believed the hostages would be released soon.

Todd joined the conversation. "They're all mental cases by now," he said. "They should commit suicide."

What could I say to that? This was only hours after Todd had been returned to the group. It was a touchy situation, and no one else in our group knew how to respond. We changed the subject. Cody's Rotary Club was setting up a carnival in the park. We talked about merry-go-rounds.

But I continued to ponder Todd's short-term departure. Our group needed all twenty-nine of us. We were a community. Each one was necessary in order to pedal into Hampton Beach in triumph — to climb the Big Horn. While Todd's disappearance had threatened our wholeness, it also drew us together, just as tight as the appreciation game had done. But did he know that? Did anyone show Todd he was important, needed, loved?

Now the group, as a whole, was attacking the Big Horn. "The first ten miles on this climb are deceptive," Helen told us as we left the plains of Lovall, Wyoming, to scale a mountain range that appeared to block our path out of town. "It won't even look like you're going up, but don't try it in a high gear. You'll burn out."

She said that last year's log described the second ten miles as an obvious upgrade. The third ten miles — well, they were switchbacks, she said, and we would have no doubts about steepness. What the log neglected to describe were the final miles just before Bald Mountain campground.

But we were only biking 37.5 miles today. It should be a snap, I thought, half-convinced and half-scared. We had already climbed Lolo, Pipestone, and Sylvan Passes. After twenty days on the road, even our most "unprepared" bikers had shaped up. I wasn't going to be intimidated and hoped they wouldn't be, either.

Michelle was getting stronger; Junior was turning fat into muscle. Ted and I had to work hard now to keep up with our clustermates. I knew every muscle in my legs was being used.

I tried to remember what I knew about the Big Horn, besides its role as a geographical barrier. Did the mountain have something to do with Custer's last stand, or was that the Little Big Horn?

Now, however, I was concerned with doughnuts and orange juice that Peg had for us at our first stop where the mountain loomed over our heads. With this first peak, the rest of the mountain disappeared. We wouldn't be able to see the next ridge until we started climbing again. I ate the snack and surveyed the view, a large portion of north central Wyoming; all of Big Horn County; Big Horn Lake; the Graybull and Shoshone Rivers; and miles of empty land beyond Lovell.

"Look how red the dirt looks from up here," I said to Barbie as I pedaled up the incline after our break.

"The view is forever," she answered. Barbie was in her usual talkative, giggly mood. Mountain-climbing was easier for her, with her small size and swim-team muscles, than battling winds on the level, or cranking down rolling hills. But we moved slowly, at Junior's pace, looked at the scenery, and talked. Barbie covered subjects from plucking chickens to making strawberry jam, and how to get yeast breads to rise. She critiqued all the TV programs that she watched at home, and then covered the ones she didn't watch.

Mike, next in the line-up, talked about his Polish relatives. "Last year my aunt went over there to visit two brothers in the Polish army," he said. "The one, a private, got drunk on something called Electrified Spirits, and the other, a major, tried to hide him from their American cousin."

We laughed over the predicament as we continued pedaling. Clusters behind us were bunching up and waiting for the "slow cluster," us, to get further ahead. Junior was using his energy for biking instead of talking, but he still slowed down to his Lolo Pass pace.

Finally we reached our lunch stop — a small park situated by a mountain stream and waterfall. We had gone twenty-three miles so far, all up, but I felt refreshed by the meal of fresh fruit salad, and the tranquil setting. I was going to make it.

A tourist, driving down the mountain with his two young children, stopped at the park. When he learned that we were cycling up, he began to laugh. "If you only knew," he began, "hahahaha — if you only knew."

The man could hardly get a sentence out of his mouth without laughing. "If you only knew what's ahead of you," he said. "Steep! Steep inclines! Oh, if you could only see it first."

His little children, dabbling in the rushing water, turned to look at their boisterous father who had taken off his visor cap and was mopping his forehead. "It's a terrible climb," the man declared. He was still laughing.

We kept assuring him that we would make it. "You probably will," he said, calling his children to the car. Serious at last, he drove off. Typical non-biker, I thought. They never can believe what we do. Some of our friends at home had asked us when we told them our plans: "What are you going to do about the mountains?"

"Go over them, of course," we answered.

We continued, taking two-and-a-half mile chunks of road at about two-and-a-half miles per hour. Sometimes Junior had to walk up the inclines, especially the 180-degree hairpin turns that seemed steep enough to require a staircase instead of pavement. When we reached the pine-tree part of the mountain we met a group of four bikers coming down, three young men and a woman. They warned us about some cows in the road ahead.

Instead of cows, we saw a young man around the next bend with a tennis racket and ball.

"You're not playing tennis up here, are you?" I asked. His car was parked off on the side.

"No."

"I didn't think so." At the rate of our speed up the hill, I could have a lengthy dialogue with him before getting out of earshot.

"Just waiting for my car to cool down."

"Oh."

"Thought I'd use the time to practice a few shots."

"Why not?" I could picture the tennis ball flying out into the valley, thousands of feet below.

Doug was riding the motorcycle that day. When he wasn't repairing bikes, he rode slowly along, next to our cluster, encouraging us to keep going. "Just a few more miles and it's flat," he would say. Or, "There's a great view after this next turn." When we arrived at a wide, flat plateau, we rejoiced in reaching the summit. We had conquered the mountain — at least that was what everyone thought.

"But where's the sign?" asked Molly.

"And the book for our signatures?"

"I want an affidavit, notarized, to prove I climbed the Big Horn," said Barbara Haya.

In our trailer, Peg had set out a box of Ritz crackers and a tub of peanut butter. My body seemed to be screaming for such a snack, cholesterol or no cholesterol. I dug each cracker into the tub, squashed a cracker lid on it, and popped it into my mouth. I kept going until I ate twelve of the crispy, salty, smooth, and rich concoctions. I'm eating like Todd does, I thought. Although I tried, I couldn't put his troubles away.

I joined in the group's self-congratulatory conversation as we admired our view of ridges and plains below: "The Big Horn wasn't so bad after all — I really didn't have any trouble — the staff psyched us up for this one."

Grabbing one more cracker sandwich, I jumped on my bike for the final stretch to Bald Mountain campground, about 9000 feet in elevation. (The top of "Baldy" is 10,042.) We started with a great descent, the sun on our backs, a cool breeze on our faces, the Wyoming panorama on our right, and promises of "just a few more miles." Then the road turned heavenward. The terrain slanted up. Ridges appeared in front of us. The air took on a rarefied quality. Great walls of granite blocked our way as we left the pine trees. The real climb was just beginning.

Here was our test of stamina, a struggle of endurance to reach our inner soul. For the first time on the trip I felt defeated by the geography. This mountain was inhumane to expect us to climb its last soaring peak after all we had been through. But the mountain didn't ask to be climbed; it was just there.

Indians, explorers, pioneers, road builders, motorists, and other cyclists before us had accepted the challenge of the mountain. I recalled an Indian camp song from a summer job when I was in college. As counselor and lifeguard at a YWCA camp, I had received a little songbook which I still kept in the piano bench at home. Now I began to sing from that book, to myself; I had no extra breath on this hill climb for singing out loud.

*God of the mountain, God of the hill, Show us Thy Spirit; Teach us Thy will.*

*God of the starlight, God of the dawn, Show us a vision; Lure us on.*

*Giver of blessings, To Thee we pray: May we be thankful, ever alway.*

*God of the starlight, God of the dawn. Show us a vision; Lure us on.*

*Lure us on! Lure us on! Lure us on!*

The song was perfect for the Big Horn challenge. I wished I could share it with the group. Sometimes, Helen asked for one of us to say or sing grace at lunchtime. Would I have the nerve to sing it? I had never sung a solo before. My voice was thin and weak, but somehow this summer, this time in my life, seemed right for trying new things. Maybe I would share my "God of the Mountains."

The Big Horn road lured us on. This path was direct, not hidden by switchback turns, ridge, or forest. It didn't make any compromises; there were no engineering niceties of long curves or gentle grades. Our path went from A to B by the shortest route, a straight line, and B was Bald Mountain.

In the late afternoon, as we hobbled toward our final ascent, the land became more barren, open, and relentless in its climb to the sky. Drivers coming down the mountain shouted, "It's not much farther," or "You're almost there."

But what did they know? They were cruising down in their cars. I was trudging up with weary muscles, rebelling against this final climb. I thought about the laughing father at lunchtime; maybe he was right. If we had only known. Our minds had been tricked by the apparent top of the mountain, and now our bodies wouldn't respond. I felt betrayed by the Big Horn. Night on Bald Mountain? I might never get there.

Doug parked his cycle ahead and ran back to where cluster two was inching along. He jogged next to Junior. "Go, go, go," he repeated. As exhausted as Junior was, he laughed and tried to squirt Doug with his water bottle.

All of us seemed equal in our desperation. Even tough Tony

admitted he was tired; he had finally "seen the hill." Inch by inch, pedal revolution by revolution, grunt by groan, we advanced. On the round, bald mountaintop ahead, I could see a snowbank, shaped like a giant apostrophe glistening in the late afternoon sun.

A few feet from the crest of the true summit of the Big Horn road, was the campground lane where we turned. The climb was over. We were home. I lined my bike up with the others, a mechanical habit now requiring no thought and little energy. I took off my water bottle and headed for a rail fence several feet away. I would rest and watch the other clusters come in.

Sitting there seemed like a permanent situation. I didn't want to get out the tent or duffles. I saw Todd pick out his large blue duffle from the pile. Everything's normal again, I thought. But I couldn't even begin to think of joining the group at the water pump, soaping up arms and legs, putting their heads under the cold stream of water. I could see Barbara Haya lathering up her long hair while someone else pumped the water; she washed her hair every day, no matter what.

I sat and watched. I appreciated Peg's diligence in having dinner ready so no one would have to help tonight. I wondered what we were having. My weariness was being engulfed by hunger. Ted's cluster arrived. "You made it, you made it," I repeated. Ted groaned as he gave me a hug.

"Let's get our stuff and put the tent up," he said. "I'm going to bed early."

Most of us were asleep by 7:30. Around 9:00 P.M. our tent swayed from a roaring, crackling thunderstorm. Ted sat up and looked out of the little tent window to see if our stakes were holding. Then he pulled his corner of the sleeping bag over his head.

I watched the designs on the tent roof as sudden lightning bursts silhouetted nearby pine trees. Shadows crisscrossed the ropes quivering flag image across side and top with each flash. A flopping, flag image was created by the towel draped on one rope. But each lightning flash was over before I could study the images. The effect was like strobe lights at a rock concert.

Thunder crackled through my body from eardrums to toes. The noise seemed more real than the air I was breathing.

Waves of rain hit the tent as the wind drove it toward us and then took it away. I was fascinated, not frightened. I was safe, secure, in our refuge from the storm. But my eyelids were heavy, and I left the storm on Bald Mountain to fall asleep.

# 12

# We Have to Get to Moorcroft Tonight

I HAD ALWAYS avoided biking in the dark; it seemed dangerous. In Moorcroft, Wyoming, we would have to pedal through an hour's worth of moonless night to get to our sanctuary for the night. Just another learning experience, I rationalized.

But first came the expected exhilaration of a good downhill. I knew what it was to fly effortlessly into the wind — something like hang gliding, or downhill skiing. Downhill biking was close to that kind of thing, and Bald Mountain was no exception.

We were sliding down the other side, with sunshine and clear skies for our early morning run. After the struggle to reach the top yesterday we now claimed the prize, the free gift of several miles of coasting.

We took the middle of our lane. Helen had suggested we do that since we would be going almost as fast as the cars. On switchback curves we needed the extra room to bank our turns. "Another thing," she warned, "leave plenty of room between each biker to avoid collisions."

But we could still communicate road hazards to the biker behind us by pointing out gravel, uneven pavement, or objects in the road. I kept one eye on the road flashing by under me, and the other on the incredible scenery rushing past, unfolding in front of me, and spreading out below. Sometimes the force of the rushing wind made my eyes water and my vision blur. Hands on brake levers began to feel cramped, but I couldn't let go and still control my speed. Still that was a slight inconvenience, compared with the sense of mastery over the mountain.

On each turn I tried to have my inside pedal up; then I leaned over into the turn, thrusting my inside knee and head in that direction. When these curves went smooth and easy, it was a sensation similar to dancing or figure-skating on ice. I was thrilled by the Big Horn descent and decided it was a good time to sing "Praise God from Whom All Blessings Flow" and "America the Beautiful." I had plenty of breath to sing out this time. With the rush of the wind no one but me could hear. This was probably, I thought, as far as I would ever go with a solo. I even wished I could yodel.

At the bottom of the mountain, it was hot. Traveling through desolation after the joy of the downhill, we were now in northeastern Wyoming, under its unrelenting sun, in front of beating winds. I felt like Lawrence of Arabia crossing the Sahara. Waves of hot air were hitting us by break time when we found respite from the fiery heat at a place called Spur Ranch.

"How did you get permission for this?" I asked Helen as my cluster wheeled into a ranch with shade trees, lawn, stables, and guest house, all nestled around a luxurious main house. In the middle were our Out-Spokin' van and trailer.

"I just asked." Helen gave a shrug and smile that seemed to say, "I can't explain these things; sometimes everything works out."

The same gratitude I felt, after twenty miles of near-desert, was written on the face of each biker turning into our "mirage." Here at Spur Ranch we could fill our water bottles and use the elegant gold-decorated bathroom. "Just go through the family room, turn right at the pool table, and another right before the master bedroom," said the young woman vacuuming a thick, white living-room carpet. Family and friends relaxed on the patio and a group chatted by the stable door, all looking like "beautiful people" from the television show "Dallas." Children and dogs romped on the lawn amidst the resting bikers. Spur Ranch was a difficult place to leave.

Our next stop was Ucross, population twenty-five. Mayor Buck, who was also storekeeper, coffeeshop owner, and gas station attendant, had thin, shoulder-length, gray hair. He offered us his visitors' book to sign.

"I signed the book last summer." Doug found his name from a year ago and sat on the stool to sign it again. Cluster two was fortunate to have Doug, I thought. An informal, casual leader, he was always ready for a water fight or rough-housing with the rowdier members — especially Junior. His good looks and genial-ity attracted the young women bikers, but he played no favorites.

Next to Doug, sitting at the counter, were two of the mayor's cronies. "Don't you get tired of pedaling?" the one with the bat-tered cowboy hat asked me.

"Sure, I get tired," I said, "but it's all worth it."

"Wouldn't be to me," said the mayor, busy selling candy bars and soda to the bikers. He ignored a potential gasoline customer who had pulled up to the single pump out front. The impatient tourist, after waiting only a few minutes, drove off.

"I think a trip like yours would be nice," said the other customer whose tee-shirt stretched across an ample midsection. "I'd do it."

"Have to train first," I warned. He nodded solemnly. As we left the isolated outpost town, the mayor winked and told us to come back again. Our next contact with a government official was with the sheriff of Campbell County, Wyoming.

"The sheriff is here to see you, Mim," Conrad announced to a roomful of bikers. We were all either stretched out on the plush Campbell carpet or draped around overstuffed furniture. The Campbell County sheriff had stopped by to check on a report phoned in earlier, when Mim had found stolen goods stashed under a bridge. Mim blushed as she told the sheriff why she was in the bushes under the bridge.

"It was an emergency stop for me," she explained. "Anyway, from the place I was, I could see way up under the bridge. There was antique furniture there — a desk, a table, some chairs." Mim, Conrad, and the sheriff stood in the entry hall adjoining the room where the rest of us watched them with half-closed eyes.

In this comfort, we watched the stolen-furniture mystery un-ravel. The sheriff continued his interrogation, taking notes. "We had a report on some furniture stolen that fits your description," he told Mim. "Now, if you'll give me directions to that bridge."

We teased Mim about being entangled with Wild West justice;

we called her a "marked woman." "Wait till the furniture thieves find out that you blew the whistle on them," Ed said. "They'll be out to get you."

We were all resting in this elegant condominium rec room because, once again, Helen had asked and we had received. As the temperature reached 100 degrees, Helen was desperate to find us a refuge for lunch. After many miles of nothing, she came to these new buildings, outside of Gilette, Wyoming. The condo manager gave Helen permission for us to eat lunch and rest in the air-conditioned room admidst new furniture and decorations such as gold artifacts, paintings, and potted plants.

"You're crazy to go out in that," the manager said as she looked out on the steaming parking lot from her cool office. "It's 103 now."

I shrugged. "We have to get to Moorcroft tonight," I said and opened the heavy outside door. The heat slammed into me like a fist.

Conrad was out there, preparing to refill the water tank. "I hate to waste this leftover water," he said. "Who wants some water dumped over them?"

"I do. I do." Conrad emptied the water tank on top of my head. The cool liquid flowed right down to my shoes. I actually shivered for an instant and felt wonderfully cool, comfortable for at least fifteen minutes until the dry heat hit me again.

Helen told us about an upcoming detour and warned us about heat exhaustion. The first stages were chills and spots before our eyes, she said, then shortness of breath. I didn't have any symptoms but after the Butte illness, I watched myself. Especially since this was a ninety-eight-mile day.

Out on the road again, we saw a pickup truck drive by. It was loaded with a desk, table and chairs. "Hey, that's Mim's furniture," I said to Barbie. I had to smile. The case of the biker and the burglar was closed. Too bad we were always on the move, I thought. I'd like to stick around and see what happens.

But we would never know. Just like the newspaper photos taken of us at Skamania, we were never in one spot long enough to follow up. We left our footprints, our stamp, some kind of impression, and were gone with the dawn. I remembered a business card that said "I may pass along this way only once, but I will try to do my best." A good code of the road.

We hit the gravel construction detour Helen had mentioned. As if that wasn't enough, we had headwinds and a hill to climb. We slipped and slid among the little rocks, dodged construction water trucks and other road equipment. If only the wind would stop. If only this hill weren't so steep. If only my bike would quit going on the sideways. If only it weren't so hot. I saw cluster four stopped on the other side of the wide highway. Ruth was sitting in the shade of a building.

Our cluster crossed over, and Ted explained, "Ruth can't get her breath."

"She had to get off her bike and walk up the hill," Kirk added.

"I don't think she'll be able to ride anymore today," Ted said.

Doug knelt down next to Ruth.

"I feel like my head is detached," she gasped. Blond and fair, Ruth's healthy glow had turned to pale ashes. I was frightened by her appearance and didn't know what to do to help her.

"Drink some salt water," Doug advised. His newest nickname was Doctor Doug, and it seemed an apt label. "That might help."

Kirk said he'd go inside the building, a liquor store, to ask for salt. He brought out a whole salt shaker and emptied it into half a bottle of water. Ruth gulped it down as we all stood around and watched. She said she felt better almost immediately.

The other clusters joined us, a milling group of hot, tired, and discouraged bikers. Helen suggested we take an hour break at a nearby park in Gilette, even though we would get behind schedule. At least we had reached the end of the eight-mile detour. As I turned my bike into the park, I saw a man in a truck watching the line of bikers.

"Where are you going?" he asked.

"New Hampshire."

"That's far."

"Too far today," I admitted, but his question lifted me out of the present, uncomfortable moment.

Peanut butter sandwiches and punch; sitting on a grassy hill in the shade; Doug playing the guitar; that was our rest. Ruth was recovering and Doug, although he looked as tired as the rest of us, led us in a renewal of spirit. The breeze that harrassed us now as we lounged in the shade. "Let's pray for God's strength," he said, "and help for those in physical pain."

Doug concluded the gathering with a secret-admirer game. We wrote the name of the biker on our right on a sheet of paper, and a compliment for that person on the other side, folded the paper, and passed it on.

Ted and I were sitting on a grassy knoll when we were given our complimentary notes to read in private. The willow branches danced overhead in the wind. I opened mine to read: "Smiles a lot. Never shows her tiredness. Compromises with the group decisions. Lets everyone know how she feels without hurting anyone." The compliments made me feel accepted, secure, part of the group, and a bit embarrassed by the kind words.

"How were yours, Ted?"

"Okay." He showed them to me: "Creative, good sense of humor, friendly, always ready to go. Drywit, fun to kid with. He tells people what he really feels, which is good. Sometimes he won't change his mind. He always says something funny and nice to me, and that makes me feel good inside. Enjoys living. An intelligent man. Enjoys challenges. I see a more caring person emerging as I get to know you better."

"These comments are terrific," I said. "Don't they make you feel good?"

Ted chuckled, "Yeah, I was surprised."

I felt like a mother who has sent a child off to kindergarten and gets back a good report. I had brought Ted along on the trip — dragged him along — and he was accepted by the gang. They had found the same endearing characteristics in him that I had, and I felt vindicated.

The winds smiled at us, too, as we continued on our way to Moorcroft two hours later. Now we had tailwinds, biking was easy, and the highway was smooth. There was little traffic, but those who passed us honked and waved as though they knew about our trials in the heat and were reinforcing us with support. One driver yelled, "Hi, Mennonites," I felt protected by the friendly people, even as we were rapidly running out of daylight.

Long shadows of cars and trucks overtaking us covered the pavement ahead of me as the sun reached the horizon. I cringed at the menacing black squares that advanced before me, and had to keep reminding myself they were only shadows. A little VW, for example, threw a shadow as huge as a truck — a dark blob engulfing several bikers ahead. A big truck's shadow was almost a block long, and traveled through us at sixty miles-per-hour. I jumped as each shadow went through me.

With one more mile to go, the dusk was heavy enough for automobile headlights. People still honked and waved; maybe they sensed the danger we were in.

Our bikes did not have lights. Although Ted and I had brought along our own leg-lights, they were in the van, not with us. All that any of us had to alert overtaking traffic to our presence were the reflectors on our pedals.

Conrad slowed his motorcycle down next to me, last in my cluster line-up. "Keep pedaling when you hear traffic behind you," Conrad told us. "That way they can see the reflectors going up and down. You're more visible. Pass the word ahead."

Helen was leading cluster three which soon caught up with us. "It's safer now for all of us to ride together," she called to me. "Then when we get to the off-ramp, we'll double up. Conrad's going to ride in back so his headlight shines on us."

It was completely dark by the time we left the highway. Street-lights, car lights, and neon signs punctuated the blackness. We rode in pairs and I strained to see obstacles on the road, as well as bikers ahead, behind, and on my side. It was an exercise in caution, and I feared a disastrous pile-up of bikes and people. We all stopped at a corner. "Braking, stopping, braking, stopping," was called out down the line.

Helen asked a motorist for directions to the church.

"First Baptist?" he repeated. "Just up this street two blocks and turn left."

"Could you follow us," Helen asked, "so we can have the safety of your car headlights?"

"Sure," the driver said. "Glad to." Once more I felt sheltered and cared for by our along-the-way neighbors.

"If this ever happens again," Helen vowed, as we reached the church safely, "I'll ask for a police escort."

"Maybe we can get the sheriff of Campbell County," laughed Mim.

# 13
# Only Accidental

OUR SILENT cycles, wheeling past ravaged canyons and eroded gorges, underlined the quiet, pastel beauty of the Badlands at dawn. My spirits were lifted; I liked the feeling that we were part of this awesome work of God's creation. And there was no automobile traffic, for we had arisen at 4:30 to beat the summer heat of the South Dakota plains.

We were at the halfway point of our trip. South Dakota was a transition state, from the West's wild, sparsely populated, mountainous, spectacular scenery, to the great prairies, grasslands, plains, and farmlands of the Midwest.

We had climbed Mount Rushmore under a threatening sky of low clouds. The sculptured heads on the mountain emerged above the trees as we pedaled closer to the landmark masterpiece. The presidents were symbolic, I understood, of four stages of our country's development: founding, expansion, preservation after the Civil War, and conservation. I sensed the spirit of America in this work of art, and it seemed right that it was located in South Dakota, a heartland state. I felt I was a pilgrim struggling up to a sculptured shrine, and I was proud to be under my own power—with every pedal, going higher and higher.

Junior's pedals were certainly going faster. He was making it up the hill twenty-five pounds lighter, as we learned from the scale in Spearfish, South Dakota. To celebrate our free day in that picturesque, western town, Out-Spokin' had treated all twenty-nine bikers to dinner at the Village Cafe.

We all wore our one-and-only "dress-up outfit." All of us expected to "pig out" at the cafe's all-you-can-eat buffet. I noticed a scale near the entrance to the dining porch. "Junior," I had called to him, "weigh yourself."

"I'll weigh, both before and after I eat," he said as he put a nickel in the slot. I looked at Junior in his clean tee-shirt and jeans. He had lost several inches around his waist. I remembered the $5 bet he had won in Wyoming for going twenty-four hours without food. I was one of his five fans who put up $1 each for his fast.

The needle on the scale swung around and rested on 225. "I lost twenty-five pounds," Junior announced.

A cheer went up from fellow bikers, assembling in line for the buffet. "What will your football coach say about your weight loss?" Doug asked as he took a plate off the stack.

"Oh, he wants me thinner, too," Junior laughed, following right behind Doug, piling on the gravy over slabs of roast beef. "At 250, I fall over too easy."

So what if Junior added another five pounds with several help-ings of mashed potatoes and gravy? He would cycle it off tomorrow. He was going to continue losing, I was convinced. I felt determined that he should get down to 200, maybe more determined than he did. But I wasn't the only one; a family friend at home had offered him $100 if he could lose 50 pounds. At any rate, Junior was definitely biking uphill better at 225.

On top of Rushmore we saw silhouetted against a hazy sky the 60-foot presidents' heads — Washington, Jefferson, Lincoln, and Theodore Roosevelt — created in solid granite by sculptor Gutzon Borglum. The memorial rose 400 feet above a viewing terrace, crowded now with tourists. Since I had seen the carvings just four years ago, I decided to explore, and followed a sign to the sculptor's studio. A young sculptor there was finishing up a head of Moses from a three-foot chunk of burnt pine. Under his National Endowment for the Arts grant, he said he would be learning to sculpt in stone, with direction from the Rushmore sculptor-in-residence. "What a wonderful place to work," I said as I peered through the large studio windows that framed the four granite heads towering against the sky.

"I'm a biker, too," the sculptor said when I told him about our trip. "Sometimes I cycle up here just for the wonderful downhill."

The mountain roads, on that wonderful downhill, were glazed by rain that had just started. I exercised extreme caution as we descended from Rushmore on dangerous, slick pavement. "There's been an accident," a woman in a car called to us when we reached the flatland. "A big pile-up of bikes, and one of the girls lost all her teeth."

Oh, no! We waited and wondered who was hurt. Our cluster had made it safely to the bottom and were "flagging" the corner. That was our signal to the cluster behind us that we were turning a corner. We would wave our orange safety flags; when they responded then we knew they had the message. But no one was coming behind us this time.

Finally, Conrad arrived on the motorcycle to confer with Doug. Their faces were grave. Doug told us the accident was in cluster five, but they didn't know yet how badly anyone was hurt. He told us to go on.

As we plodded on to the next rest stop, I mentally checked off the women members of cluster five — Barbara Haya, Peg, and Tracy. Who had lost all her teeth? I felt a chill over my whole body at the thought.

At the next stop we learned that Barbara Haya had skidded and fallen face-down on the hill. She had broken her two front teeth. Not Barbara, I fumed. I felt close to our fellow Californian. She was on this trip because of me. Barbara had been one of the original people who answered my ad. When I had told her about Out-Spokin', she signed up, too. I felt responsibility for her being here.

Peg had run into Barbara for the second spill, and the third member of the cluster pile-up was Dave Lapp, the leader. He had turned his head when he heard the commotion behind him, and slipped. He was apparently unhurt, but Helen was worried about a possible concussion for Peg. Doug told us she had taken both of the young women to the emergency room of the hospital.

Just the word emergency scared me. Like most parents, we had taken our children on several quick trips to the hospital for cut chins and head wounds. Ted was always better in such emergencies than I. My part in these dramas was usually staying at home with the other children, and praying, just as I prayed now for Barb and Peg.

At dinnertime, they came back to us, scraped and sore but basically okay except for the lost-forever pieces of Barbara's teeth. "I saw little white fragments on the black asphalt," Barbara said, "and I knew they were my teeth."

A jagged, snaggled grimace had replaced Barbara's gracious toothpaste-ad smile. I wished she could have replayed that downhill trip and somehow avoided the fall. How quickly things can change; how suddenly we can lose our appearance, or that "magical" protection we sometimes think we have. After all, God never promised us immunity from pain, but strength to overcome.

"If I told my mother, she'd be just sick and tell me to come home right away," Barbara sighed. We all stood around our injured member and heard her story. "I'll wait and tell her after I get permanent caps in Boston."

Peg was feeling better and would rest the next day, just to be sure, and Helen had made an appointment with a Rapid City dentist. Barbie, who had broken a piece of her braces during mealtime a few days earlier, would go to the dentist at the same time.

That meant that the next morning, as my cluster faced a rolling-hill terrain, we would be a small group—only Junior, Sherm, Mike, and me. Doug was riding the motorcycle. It was me and the three eighteen-year-olds as lead cluster for the day.

Junior, hyped for action, asked to be our leader. Mike, who always moved right along, was next; then Sherm, who had recently accelerated his usual good pace; and I was last. I could tell this for certain, as we flew with a bunch of speedsters. I could tell this for certain, as we flew down the highway with early-morning energy to the Skyline Drive turn-off. We had moved so fast we had to wait 20 minutes before we could flag the corner for cluster three.

Such energy. We circled on the quiet road as we waited. Junior did figure eights and Sherm tried some skids and wheelies. Mike lazily went up and down a rise in the road. "I'm really working to stay up with you guys," I reminded them. "I'm not complaining; I like it."

We were all hot shots today in cluster two, scorchers, out to conquer the hills and whatever else the day held for us.

Soon we were sweeping across Skyline Drive, along the spine of a ridge overlooking Rapid City, South Dakota. I followed behind Sherm, both of us anxious to tackle the next stretch of road to Dinosaur Park. The suburban road was narrow and curvy, lined with view houses facing the prairie flatlands below. Skyline's curves were sharper than most of the roads we had encountered on the trip, and its sudden steepness often came as a surprise. The road reminded me of the descent from the Griffith Park Observatory in Los Angeles and the stories I had heard of experienced riders who slipped on its wet pavement or patches of sand. I spent weeks on that road practicing downhill maneuvers.

Flying down an S-curve now on Skyline Drive, however, was another story. I began to wonder if I could stay on my side of the road. I was afraid I was going too fast for the unbanked curve. The momentum threw me out into the opposing lane. I couldn't see around the corner and I panicked. I was close to the edge now, past the literal edge of my lane, and the figurative edge of disaster. I applied more brakes and tried to shift the center of balance by throwing my weight into the curve. A garbage truck had passed us earlier, but the road was empty now as I came around the bend.

Sherm was flying down ahead of me, shooting way ahead, going into the second half of the "S." As he hit a patch of gravel at the outside edge of the curve, his bike turned sideways. He slammed down onto the pavement, sliding on the gravel for at least fifteen feet.

"Sherm!"

I squeezed my brake levers as hard as I could without throwing myself in a heap on top of his bike. A big dog from the house on the hill started down the driveway, barking at us. "Get home, you mutt," I snarled. The dog backed off. "Sherm, are you okay?"

I could see a triangular area, blood red, on the outside of his thigh, from the fringe of his cut-off jeans to his knee. Sherm must have scraped off several layers of skin as his leg was dragged through the gravel at top speed. I threw my bike against the hillside, grabbed my bandanna and water bottle, and ran to him. "Here, can you use these?"

Sherm was inspecting the damage. Cluster three appeared at the top of the hill, approaching the descent. "Take it slow," I yelled. "It's dangerous. Sherm has fallen. Go slow."

I wished we had a signal that meant "Danger, look out," I didn't want them to fall, too, but they couldn't hear what I was saying. Just seeing Sherm lying on the pavement was message enough. They slowed and stopped.

"What happened to you, Sherm?"

"That looks awful."

"Shall we get Helen?"

Then we all remembered. Helen and the van weren't around this morning because they were at the dentist with the two Barbaras. I was trying to remember those first-aid courses I had taken, those articles on what-to-do in emergencies. I was wishing I hadn't always taken the easy way out with our kids when they were injured, so I'd have some experience now.

"I'll just ride to the park," Sherm said, "and clean it up there. I'll be okay." The color was gone from his tanned face. Brown eyebrows and hair looked darker than usual.

"Are you sure?" I asked. Sherm winced as he tried to pick out some of the gravel from his wound. The pain must have been fierce. I must be looking right at his muscle, I thought.

I didn't know what I should do; none of us did. Our R.N., Mim, was in cluster one, last in the line-up today. Sherm just wrapped my bandanna around the wound and got on his bike. He stoically pedaled the remaining few miles to Dinosaur Park.

"Doctor" Doug was there on the motorcycle. He got out his first-aid kit and took the injured rider into the men's room.

Only minutes before, our cluster had been confident and high-spirited; now we were plunged into gloom. A fellow rider had fallen and been seriously injured. I had often heard Sherm say that he tried to learn from experiences in life. "It's that way with a lot of things," he had said. "I have to suffer first before I learn."

Doug had put peroxide on the wound and covered it with bandages. Sherm insisted on riding. I was leery; it looked like a major injury to me. But Sherm didn't give up easily. Early in the trip he said that he wanted to become close again to the Lord this summer. Though it may not be happening the way he had planned it, his request was being granted.

Our route followed a level, four-lane divided highway that had little traffic. Since the road's shoulder was rough, we rode on the edge of the "slow" lane. Sherm said the wound hurt only when his bike was jostled.

A South Dakota state trooper, with a sign "Operation Care" on his station wagon, drove by with lights flashing and pulled us over. "Does he mean us?" I wondered aloud as the state car stopped. "Is he going to give us a ticket?" Mike laughed as the trooper walked toward us.

"There's a $27 minimum fine for traveling at less than 40 miles per hour on the freeway," he said. "You'll have to ride on the shoulder."

The trooper's hat reminded me of the one worn by Smokey the Bear. "Twenty-seven dollars for each of us?" I asked. That would be over $700 for the whole troupe, I figured; it wasn't a laughing matter after all.

"Yes, but I'll let you off," he said, "if you start riding on the shoulder right now."

We pointed out how rough the cracked pavement was. "You have to ride there even if it is rough," he insisted. "What's a little scrape?"

We looked at Sherm. He didn't admit to the pain but his sore was bubbling and draining. What's a little scrape? What's a big scrape? I wanted to show that state trooper.

"What's a little scrape," the trooper continued, "compared to a complete wipe-out on the road from a big truck?"

There was no answer to that. No point in arguing. We would ride on the bumpy shoulder. Mercifully, the surface of the shoulder improved and Sherm was more comfortable. At our next stop Helen, back from the dentist trip, said she would purchase some salve for his wound and see about a doctor at the first large town. Wall, South Dakota's Wall Drugstore town, was coming up, but that didn't necessarily mean they had a pharmacy.

We had seen the Wall Drugstore signs several states away. Wall was a well-advertised, internationally publicized mecca offering free ice water, original oil paintings, a six-foot rabbit, old coin collections, free coffee and doughnuts for honeymooners, and nickel coffee for everyone. Our campground was just across the railroad tracks from Wall's main street, a combination of Knott's Berry Farm and Hollywood's Farmer's Market.

After dinner, as Ted and I searched for the nickel coffee, we saw Ed and Chip touring the town. Ed told us, "We had dinner in an Italian restaurant." He was proud of his Italian heritage and promised to cook spaghetti for the group as soon as he got his mom's recipe.

The longer we were away from home, the more I thought Ed looked like our son. I suppose that was a sign I missed Matt and was getting homesick.

"We're supposed to be grounded," Chip said. The bright prairie sun was setting and turning the western fronts of Wall's main street into a vivid, unreal stage setting as we stood there talking. "We are wondering what our rights are," Ed asked. "What did we sign anyway?"

"You'd think this was basic training for the Army," Chip said.

"Helen even threatened to send us home," Ed added with a frown. I couldn't believe it. "What did you do?"

"I missed devotions."

"And you were caught throwing rocks during quiet time."

"I kept the whole group waiting a few times."

"You refused to do the morning warm-up games."

"But the worst is that both of us have been seen in places that sell beer."

Ted and I went on to our nickel coffee and apple pie, discussing the Ed and Chip crisis. Why did those two always remind me of the Little Rascals or Our Gang?

Chip's real name was Hervey, named for his father and grandfather, which made him Hervey the Third. But his mother didn't like the name Hervey, he had explained, and called him Chip. He was a tall, lanky guy with white-blond hair, a good, strong biker, and Ted's clustermate. "Chip reminds me of myself at that age," he had said.

Sending them home sounded too harsh, Ted and I agreed, and grounding sounded a little juvenile. They were twenty years old and weren't schoolboys. But were they acting like "bad little kids"?

Another surprise storm struck in the middle of the night. As our tent strained at ropes and stakes, I could hear Mim giggling nearby. The tent she was sharing with Linda and Michelle had just collapsed on top of them. During the height of the howling winds and rain, with several bikers out fighting the elements, flapping nylon, and errant ropes, I heard someone say, "I want my mommy." Some of these kids are getting homesick, I thought. That's part of the problem.

At Girl Scout camp, when I was twelve, one of my tentmates had called out in the middle of the night for her mother. What a baby, I thought. I had signed up for two more weeks after the first session was over, but during that fourth week I remember feeling sick to my stomach and generally unhappy. Homesickness had hit me, too.

This was our fifteenth day on the road, thirty eight to go. For some of our fellow cyclists, we were a long way from their homes, whether they were in Indiana, Pennsylvania, or California. I for one felt the distance in time and miles. But even more than going home, I wanted to see what lay ahead, around the next bend of the road. So did Barbara Haya and Sherm, as they rode with us once again.

We cycled eight miles to the entrance to Badlands National Park in a quiet dawn of clear skies and light breeze. Red-and-white striped mountains introduced our twenty-two-mile tour through the varicolored, irregular ravines and canyons. Rain had intensified the colors radiating back at us. Our silent line of bikers slipped in and out of yellow, green, and orange canyons reminiscent of the Grand Canyon.

I saw grotesque formations of earth near the road, and then looked out over the stark vista of ridges, all dramatized by morning shadows. We were on the moon, or another planet, and I was happy to be there — to be on this trip — to be alive.

The day was beginning to heat up at 8:00 A.M. when we stopped at one of the viewpoints. Tourists in cars had now joined the parade, and one woman said to me, "We were in Wall last night and there was a terrible storm."

"I know," I said. "We were there, too." I could see a look of disbelief on her face. How could we have arrived here by bicycle so soon? People who were not familiar with bicycle touring were constantly amazed at our mileage. The first time I told my mother about the 450-mile two-week tour in Oregon, she wrote back, "That must be a mistake. Don't you mean 45 miles?"

Another group of tourists was speculating about us: "Everyone in the group is young except those two. They must be the leaders. What a lot of responsibility they have." Ted and I were often misidentified as supervisors, van drivers, cooks, or visiting parents, or grandparents. We corrected the mistaken impressions; we were bikers, just like the rest.

Helen, only twenty-two years old, was our leader. She had the responsibility, the duties that included emergency hospital trips, dentist appointments, medical care for the wounded, searches for lost bikers, and enforcement of rules. As coordinator, Helen tried to please everyone, to answer all questions and complaints. She rose in the morning before anyone else, and was often the last one to retire, but always had a smile and cheery outlook. She and the other three staffers did it all as volunteer workers. They were only paid $25 a month; their commitment was priceless.

But maybe it was time I took some responsibility, too, I thought. Maybe I should quit thinking that my neighbor was only someone along the way; Vicki Turner with a flat tire, or the owner of the stolen furniture. My neighbor was in our group, too. Some of them were hurting, and I had better start loving them.

# 14
# No Water Bottle for Todd

THE SOUTH DAKOTA water tasted odd, too full of minerals, flat, and muddy. Sometimes it had a lead-pencil taste. But water, in one way or other, was playing a big role in our South Dakota tour.

Some of the bikers just refused to drink this water. They said they would rely on buying soda at our breaks. Todd was especially vehement in his rejection of the water. "It's too bad to drink," he told Helen. "I bet *you* wouldn't drink a whole bottle full of it."

Before the week was out, Todd's water bottle would be symbolic of the standoff between Helen and him. Their relationship seemed to be one of baiting, testing, give and take, with an edge of sarcasm on Todd's part. Helen appeared resigned to the role of "authority figure," someone for Todd to needle and challenge.

"There's nothing wrong with the water, Todd," Helen answered him.

"I'll bet you $3 you won't drink it down — a whole bottle, all at once," Todd taunted her.

"I bet I will." Sparks flashed from Helen's dark eyes. There was something commanding about her. Although she was average in size, her excess energy and strength gave her leadership quality. She claimed she walked like a farmer. "And look at my hands," she would say. "That's a farmer's hand, a worker's hand." She liked rough-and-tumble play, water fights, and active games. Now she laughed and picked up her water bottle. "Watch this."

With everyone gathered around, amidst cries of "Ugh!" and "How can you?" she finished off the entire contents of her water bottle. I was surprised. A whole bottle! I could only gulp down a

124

few swallows at a time. Helen proved her point to Todd that the water was drinkable and collected his $3.

Much of the water in central South Dakota came from warm artesian wells. We were now approaching Philip, where this water was being used for heating buildings. Philip, situated in an apparently benign tree-shaded valley ahead, was often singled out as the hottest and coldest city in the U.S., depending upon the season. Clouds hanging over the town now gave it some shade, so it looked better than the plains where we had been biking all day with no cloud cover.

Philip looked inviting, and we had been looking at it for a long time. Every landmark in this prairie land took hours to reach, even after we first glimpsed it on the horizon. The landscape recalled to me a Bicentennial rider's description of Kansas: "We saw a speck on the horizon in the morning. At noon we could tell it was a grain elevator. At night we were there." I was learning that South Dakota was also a long, flat state requiring eight days for us to get through.

As we started the long, gradual downhill leading to Philip, I saw dozens of black skidmarks. Probably from hot-rodders wheeling down the hill, I thought. The skids looked like black ribbons, winding back and forth across the pavement, twisting and turning, sometimes doubling back, or going off the road at places, but always pulling us down the hill to Philip.

"The town has really welcomed us," Helen told the group when we assembled at the high school, our sleeping quarters for the night. "We can use the showers here in the gym and we are guests of the town at their swimming pool. The president of the Junior Chamber of Commerce also told me to pick out food in the grocery store for our dinner and give the bill to them."

"Whoopee."

"Steak tonight."

"Better than that," said Helen. "Banana splits."

The people in Philip were friendly, from those strolling by on the sidewalk, or neighbors sitting on their front porches nodding to us as we went by, to locker room attendants at the pool. The next morning a young construction worker, Randy, stopped to talk to Ted before starting work at the high school. He said they were converting the school's heating system to natural energy by using 165-degree water from artesian wells located three thousand feet underground. Ted traded stories about the solar sodium tower being developed by his own company.

I joined the two as soon as I finished my breakfast. We sat on the pipe fence in the school parking lot. Randy said his grandparents owned a "small" sixty-thousand-acre farm in the area. He offered Ted a pinch of snuff from the small tin he carried in his pocket.

"No, thanks," Ted said. "I never got into that."

Snuff? I had only seen that in ads, or old movies. I was fascinated and watched how Randy handled it. The young man, who seemed to be about twenty years old, took a small piece and placed it between his lower lip and front gum. As he talked, he regularly spit the juice generated by the snuff onto the ground. It seemed strange to me, but I suppose people can get used to anything.

We talked about the nice people in Philip. "We're humbled by our weather," Randy said, "just got to be friendly here."

Our hot, sticky, parched, artesian-well-watered day ended with a downhill again. We were heading toward another tree-shaded city, Pierre, situated on the Missouri River. Pronounced *pere*, as the residents told me, Pierre was also the capital of South Dakota. We were camping in a large city park by the river. The park had a swimming pool, and band shell where a concert would be held that night. But time for these diversions was tight with dinner, clean-up, and devotions to squeeze in before bedtime.

I put my swimsuit on under my clothes to save time. As soon as our evening gathering was over, I planned to run across the lawn, past the band concert which was now in full tune, and take a swim and shower.

Tonight we were writing letters to God, Doug announced as he handed out paper. Without hesitating, I wrote, "Dear God, help me from being bored with devotions, songs, people, and wanting to get through with it and away." After a few more sentences, I was ready to go. I was afraid I was being flippant with something that could be meaningful, but I was being honest. That was what I was feeling right then. I was hurting; I needed escape; I wanted some physical comforts.

The others seemed to be writing and writing and writing. Doug extended our ten minutes to fifteen. I could hear applause from the concert audience and then another oom-pah number. Such a pleasant, restful, relaxing way to spend a warm summer evening, and I was missing it. Music was definitely one of God's blessings; I should have written that in my letter.

I just didn't want to be here, sitting on scratchy grass, in my swim suit and wilted brown dress. Over the concert music were shrieks from swimmers jumping into the pool. Swimming at night was a childhood delight I remembered from torrid St. Louis summers. The lighted pool at Shaw Park in Clayton, with its canopy-covered stand for spectators, had been my favorite.

Now another five minutes passed before Doug had everyone's attention. "Who would like to share their letter?" he asked.

I closed my eyes and wiggled my bare feet. The delay was unbearable; I would not participate in this torture. It was more than I could endure. If I couldn't go to the concert — if I couldn't go swimming — at least I could have a shower. Filtered through my seething anger, I heard snatches of letters shared. The bikers had written about safety, health, and the beauty of life, but I couldn't appreciate any of it. With the last amen, I bolted for the pool, with Ted one-half step behind me.

A quick inspection of our respective dressing rooms and we knew the truth — there were no showers. A swimming-pool dressing room without any showers?

I asked the attendant. "No showers," she said.

I didn't bother to ask why not.

Ted and I plunged our hot, sticky bodies into the crowded, tepid pool for a quick dip. Then we walked back to camp along the river. "I wonder how many of the kids are really aware that the Missouri River is only a few blocks from our campsite?" Ted asked.

"We should have had devotions on the river bank," I answered. "That sort of thing would combine the program with some local color." I felt ashamed of my attitude during the evening gathering, but wondered if others might not feel the same way. I believed in making worship attractive, alluring, pleasant, something to look forward to, a comforting respite from trials of the day. I remembered what a friend had said when she was explaining her daily meditation: "It's not that I think to myself, 'Oh, I have to meditate now,' but it's more like, 'Now I *get* to meditate.'"

That's the way I have felt about worship — it is a privilege, an opportunity, an invitation from the Lord. So I was surprised to find myself agreeing with Ted in his objections to "compulsory chapel." I always liked campfire programs. One summer I went to three one-week church camps. I loved to sing and delve into my faith along with fellow campers.

But to schedule a meeting, such as tonight, against prime-time activities seemed an exercise in frustration to me. I felt more at peace with God and His universe by walking along the Missouri River, with Ted at my side, than I had for several days.

But I also saw myself becoming a rebel, in spite of my intentions to be a servant. I certainly wasn't Mama; I was the "mean little kid."

Our next-day's schedule called for the trip's first church-provided dinner, at Wayne and Mildred Miller's, near Miller, South Dakota. Of course, I wanted to be there, so I quit being a rebel. I arose before dawn with all the rest. By noon we were humbled again by the weather, as Randy had said in Philip.

When Junior emptied his water bottle onto his bare back, the drops seemed to sizzle in the heat, sending off "sparks" of dust. "Junior," I yelled, "the water does more good inside." But Junior didn't like the taste any more than the rest of us did.

Doug had called for a water-drinking cluster break on the road's shoulder, to encourage more consumption of water because of the dry heat. I tried a few dried-out raisins washed down by the last drop of artesian-well water in my bottle. But the idea of water on the outside was appealing. Looking along our route, an empty straight line to the horizon, I saw a glistening of water in the field next to the road. Only a fence separated us from a giant irrigation sprinkler, at least 500 feet in length, that was showering the farmer's young crop of corn with cascades of water.

"Hey, Doug, let's take a real water break," I shouted, leaping off my bike and heading for the open gate. "We won't hurt the plants." Doug hesitated an instant, and then all five of us had helmets and riding gloves off and were running toward the water.

We turned our faces up to the spray, let it trickle down our necks and inside our shirts, soak our biking shorts, and stream down our legs. The spray washed the dust off the bare-chested guys and made rivulet-designs on their gritty backs. Salt-caked skin felt clean again; sweaty, matted hair was rinsed; and fingers numbed from gripping handlebars relaxed in the zinging droplets.

We picked our way through corn rows to a downpour caused by a leaky connection to wash our sun-parched arms and necks. We were dancing, praising the gift of water. During our most celebrative maneuvers, a horn-tooting camper sped by on the highway with all members of the family waving at us. They must have seen our bikes at the side of the road and understood our joy.

When the frenzy of the water folly was over, we shivered a little. "What a mess," Barbie called out as she noticed mud building up on our shoes. The wet sticky ooze grew into increasingly bulky masses as we clodded through the mud to the road.

Just the price we have to pay, I thought, as we vigorously scraped away the clods. I felt renewed by our shower. Even those hateful headwinds felt glorious now. Dry breezes caressed our wet clothes and bodies, giving us the impetus to endure a little longer. The artesian-well water was super for a shower.

As the day of heat and headwinds, sometimes whistling a tune in the headset of my bike, drew to a close, I was groggy. If I wasn't actually sleeping while pedaling, I was at least in a hypnotic trance. I stared at my long shadow out on the road in front of my bike and had to laugh. That woke me up; the round helmet made me look like a little combat soldier.

Out of the combat at last, we reached the oasis-paradise of the Millers' farmhouse, a reality with shade trees, friendly faces, guest cars in the driveway, and a sumptuous buffet set out under the trees. Mrs. Miller, with silver-rimmed glasses and braided hair, was a gracious neighbor welcoming us to her home, an efficient hostess, and the sweet-faced mother we all needed after seventy eight miles of South Dakota weather. Equally generous was Wayne Miller, a prosperous farmer sharing his home and yard with us biking pilgrims.

Church friends, gathered from thirty miles around, brought food and good wishes. We talked and ate our way through three helpings of chicken, beans, vegetables, salads, iced tea, cookies, brownies, and seven different kinds of homemade pie. The evening concluded with informal sharing of songs and ideas. I mentioned my dream of "more bikes than cars." "Especially in

Yellowstone," I told the group. "They should ban everything except bikers and hikers — maybe have tramways for the rest of the people."

"That probably didn't go over so well," Ted said to me as we settled down in our sleeping bag under the backyard elm. "Didn't you notice all those campers, trucks, and big cars in the driveway?" The next morning the Millers served us a huge breakfast. Assembled in their formal dining room at a table that comfortably seated fourteen of us at a time, we seemed like long-lost adopted children. We were overwhelmed with good humor and scrambled eggs, juice, fresh milk, five choices of cereal, and large, five-inch Danish pastries.

I looked at the Miller family photographs, beveled mirrors, and paneled wainscoting on the walls, and beyond into their homey, gracious living room, and thought of the many family gatherings those rooms had seen. I had always wanted to visit a farm when I

**The Millers of South Dakota join the bikers in morning warm-up exercises.**

was a child, but we didn't have a single relative who lived in the country. We didn't even know anyone on a farm. Finally, when I was about twelve, I had a chance to spend a weekend with my friend Betty at her relative's farm. I still have the picture marking my first time on a horse. There's a terrified look on my face and my arms are clinging around that placid animal's neck.

After the Miller's, our first stop was at a deserted one-room schoolhouse set in the middle of a field. Next to the square school building were two outhouses, open and available for use.

We also looked into the windows of the locked schoolhouse to see desks, bookshelves, and blackboards all still in place. As we scrambled about, looking in cracks and trying doors and windows, Todd gave a hard pull on a door, breaking a hinge.

"Now we can get in," he said. But the door wouldn't open wide enough, and it was time to get back on our bikes. The broken hinge hanging there on one nail looked pathetic.

At our next stop I noticed Todd standing by his bike in the sun, while the rest of the group rested in the shade of the van and trailer.

"What's the matter, Todd?"

"Nothing."

I saw that his water bottle was not on his bike and asked him about it.

"Helen took it."

"Why? Because you don't like the water?"

"No. Because I wouldn't leave the $5."

"What are you talking about?"

"You know the hinge I broke at the schoolhouse? Helen said I should leave $5 in an envelope to repair it. I wouldn't do it, so she took my water bottle until I repay the five dollars she left there."

I looked at Todd standing there, resolute, jaw clenched in determination, staring into space. The sun was blazing at both of us from a cloudless sky; dry air whipped around us, radiating additional heat from the asphalt parking lot. "I wouldn't send anyone out on a bike without a water bottle today," I said. "You want to borrow mine?"

"No. I'm not going to drink any water, or anything."

My cluster was calling me to leave. Maybe at the next break, I thought, I could just put my water bottle on his bike without saying anything. I had several cans of juice in my bike bag.

But should I interfere? Was it any of my business? Yet I had decided to start taking on some responsibility. Todd is hurting, isn't he; and he is my brother, isn't he?

# 15

# Another Way Out

WE DIDN'T REALIZE at first that our visitors in Montevideo, Minnesota, represented a tempting opportunity for Ted and I to leave the group. It could be a graceful way for us to exit, if we wanted to. Ted's sister Doris and her husband, Bob, lived only sixty miles from our route, in Glenwood, where Ted grew up, and they drove down to see us.

Helen had tried to reroute the whole group when she learned how close we would be to Ted's hometown. "I've always said I married Ted for his hometown," I told Helen. "It's a beautiful place." But there seemed to be no way to ring it in because our Minnesota schedule called for two 100-mile-plus days. It would have been fun to bicycle down Glenwood's main street, but there was just no way. Besides, first we had to get out of South Dakota.

It was our eighth day in that state and riding conditions in cluster two were driving me wild. It was stop and start, slow down and pedal fast, stop and start, until my frustrations were equal to Ted's.

Riding every day in our clusters, eight hours more or less, was almost like a daily job. In order to enjoy the "work," I felt I had to give my best effort. But how could I? Barbie was slowing all our downhills and Junior was slowing down on the uphills. I felt like a yo-yo.

Today my patience with Barbie's lagging, low-energy riding completely gave out. Everything I had been suppressing boiled to the surface. "I'm going to strangle her if she doesn't do better than this," I muttered into the wind as, once again, we lost the momentum from our downhill. Junior was barreling down, but

Barbie, unable to keep up the pace, thwarted us every time. I was completely baffled by the phenomenon.

And yet, when we really exhorted Barbie, she could be a powerhouse. When Mike, Sherm, Doug, even Junior, and I kept after her, she pushed for a short time. Then the spurt was over. I had to keep reminding myself of her ability, like that first day in Lincoln City when she steamed ahead. The mystery of Barbie's "rubber band" riding haunted me, and riled me, and erupted. After one full month of struggling, I felt violent.

At our morning break I found solitude to work out my feelings by a South Dakota lakeshore, down a short path from the road. Sitting on a log, I tried to let the serenity of tree-lined Cottonwood Lake, with its sun-sparkled ripples, calm my rebellious thoughts. I searched for God's peace.

I kept coming back to the idea that I needed to blow off steam at the end of each day. I had to escape all the rules and regulations, plus the constant pushing of Barbie and Junior that was our cluster's lot. Maybe I needed more time alone. Our fifteen-minute quiet time each morning never seemed to be long enough. Attending a devotional program in the evening when I was boiling with resentment, as I had been in Pierre, wasn't fair to anyone. As I was deciding to talk to Helen, Ted came down the path through the weeds.

"I knew you'd be here," he said, "when I saw everybody else sitting on the road. I figured you would find something better than that."

"And I did, didn't I?" I smiled. "I've also come to a decision. I'm not going to devotions tonight. I don't care what happens."

"If I have to go, you have to go," Ted laughed.

"Do you think they'll ground me, or send me home?" I laughed, too, but I was serious about my resolve.

Back at the van, I asked Helen if Ted and I couldn't be excused from the evening programs. "They're aimed at younger members," I said. "It's nothing against Doug. I could have an enjoyable philosophical or theological discussion with him anytime — in fact, we do while biking. But I don't get anything out of the programs, especially after a hectic eight- or ten-hour day on the road."

"It gets pretty bad, doesn't it?" Helen's eyes showed understanding.

"Sometimes," I confessed, "I feel like I want to strangle Barbie."

Helen didn't even look shocked. She seemed to understand my frustrations. "I wondered how long you could take it," she said. "I knew something had to give, sooner or later."

I was taken back. Helen knew all along what I was going through. I felt my problems melt away. But our break was over and clusters were getting ready to go. Helen said she would check back with me at lunchtime.

I went out on the road feeling relieved. I had confessed my worst thoughts and Helen wasn't even surprised. She seemed to have expected it all along. Even though I had been brought to a point of contemplating violence, even that could be accepted and ironed out.

As I pedaled, I looked back on the upbringing of our children and moments when I had been brought to the edge of an abyss by their behavior. I had once pictured myself hitting one of my daughters with the rail of her bunk bed; I had actually raised a bottle to clobber the other one. I hadn't done those things but realized there may be only a razor's edge of difference between anger and outright violence. I thank God for the restraint that always kept me from slipping into those murky depths.

In spite of our raging impulses, God loves us. *In spite of. Even though.* Those were important concepts, I realized, in my relationship with God and neighbor. Now all I had to do was live out those beliefs.

All? Compared to that, Lolo Pass was a snap.

"I feel terrible sometimes," Helen said as she settled on the grass next to me after lunch, "telling you and Ted what to do. I can see the irony of it because of our age difference. And you've been very good sports. I really appreciate your cooperation and help. Junior never could have made it up those mountains without your patience.

"Lots of times," Helen continued, "I have considered asking your advice about things, like disciplining Ed and Chip, and when Todd ran away. I've made a lot of mistakes. If I had some things to do over again, I'd do them differently. It's tough. I can't seem to satisfy everyone. Some days I don't satisfy anyone. But I'm trying."

I looked at the peaceful James River flowing by our lunch stop in the park, as Helen discussed the need for our group to come together each evening for cohesiveness. In theory I agreed, but in practice, I could only report my negative feelings. She said a compromise might be worked out about compulsory devotions. It could be a two-part session, the second part being voluntary Bible study. I was relieved that I wouldn't have to start a boycott or mutiny; I felt uneasy in the role of rabble-rouser.

I also suggested changing clusters, maybe just for a day, so we could ride with other members of the group. Helen smiled, her brown eyes sparkling again. "I've thought of that — a random-cluster day when names are drawn out of a hat. We'll do it once a week."

After eight windy and hot days in South Dakota, we were in Ted's home state, and our cluster cheered as we passed the Minnesota sign. However, the land of sky blue waters gave us wind and rain. We trudged through a downpour, thunder, lightning, along with headwinds. My flapping poncho, spread out like a sail, added to the wind resistance as the rain poured over me. It splashed up from the road, too, and I felt like I was back in college swimming with six lanes of thrashing swimmers.

Twenty-nine wet and bedraggled bikers herded into a wooden shelter in Montevideo's Lagoon Park at the end of a tough day, as our visitors drove up. Ted and I clambered into the back seat of Doris and Bob's car, and into a different environment. Rain and accompanying discomforts were out there, but inside were friendly faces, warm greetings, soft plush upholstery, and snacks. We munched on raspberries from Doris's garden, cut-up carrots and celery, and dry-roasted nuts, as we exchanged family news.

Doris and Bob, older than us by twenty years, were retired and spent their time keeping up with grandchildren, golf, social activities, and wintering in Texas. Over the years we had eaten many meals at their home during Glenwood vacations. Doris had even taken care of Matt when he was five months old so the rest of us could go boating in Canada. After Ted and I changed into dry clothes we all went out to a full course wall-eyed pike dinner. The four of us enjoyed renewing our close ties.

"Why don't you come home with us tonight?" Bob suggested as we lingered over coffee at the restaurant. "We'll drive you down to St. Cloud tomorrow where you can catch up with your group. You'll only miss one day."

What a tempting, outrageous suggestion. Could they see we were suffering from bone-aching weariness, marrow-chilling exposure? Did we look that bad? I didn't know it showed. Actually, I hardly ever had a chance to even look into a mirror.

But here was my chance to be free of Barbie and Junior and the constant rules and regulations of group living — for one day — or for good. The idea made me tingle. I yearned to be a free spirit, to cycle down the road at my own speed, to start and stop when I pleased, and to bicycle through Glenwood; to see any "Old Faithfuls" that we came close to.

But I'd miss Doug's conversation. Mike's stories of Polish relatives and plans for his future. Watching Sherm's wound heal and his maturity grow. Yes, I would even miss Barbie's giggles, commentary, and unfailing good humor. And Junior's good will, and my cheerleader role of encouraging his weight loss. There'd be no more happy wake-ups by Helen, or cookies by Peg, or fixed bikes by Conrad.

But really, why did I want to stay? Wasn't the thunderstorm enough? The mosquitoes? The slow riders? Regimentation? Would anyone in their right mind stay on? What kept me in this group?

Was it the friends I had made — Mim and Ruth, Ed and Chip, Helen and Doug, Barbara Haya and Molly? I could go on and on. And that's what I wanted to do, go on. I couldn't leave the job unfinished, abandon my "family," reject the spirit of love that bound us more tightly than anything we signed or agreed to. I just wanted to pedal into Hampton Beach in a glorious, triumphant parade with my group.

Besides, I had talked to Helen and we were going to try out various solutions to the problems together. The group was now my responsibility, too. They were my brothers and sisters in Christ. I couldn't quit.

We thanked Bob and Doris for a great mini-holiday and tiptoed into the darkened shelter, groping about for sleeping bags and duffles. Ted found our flashlight to help us squeeze into the line-up of sleeping bodies, but he couldn't find something else he needed.

Helen, whose sleeping bag was next to mine, whispered, "What are you looking for, Ted?"

His voice was husky above the combined snoring and night sounds of more than twenty sleeping bikers. "The toilet paper."

I stifled a giggle as Helen directed him to the elusive roll. Where else could we find such a life? I was back home where I belonged.

# 16

## On Wisconsin

THE PEACE of northern Wisconsin was a quiet interlude for us. It was the calm before the storm of the urbanized East, silence before the rumble of dynamite and Michigan trucks.

We left Minnesota by crossing the St. Croix River, just above the place where it empties into the Mississippi River. "On Wisconsin," I sang out as we crossed the bridge, getting braver with my solo singing. Some unseen fishermen on the river bank below us cheered in answer to my musical salute.

But the singing hit some sour notes. At first, on into Wisconsin meant biking on a concrete-sectioned road. Every thirty feet or so there was a two-inch jolting crack. Motorists hear a little rhythmic thump, thump, thump "song of the road" as the tires roll from section to section. To a biker, those cracks are bone-jarring tremors.

Each time my bike bridged the gap, I felt the quake from helmet, to pelvis, to the bones in my feet. For railroad tracks, I usually stood up on the pedals to avoid any jolt, but these cracks came along too frequently for that. I would look like I was riding a horse English style. Nothing seemed to help the jolt, jolt, jolt that was beginning to give me an aching back. I decided to ask Conrad to try raising my handlebars. If a toe-clip exchange helped Ted, maybe a handlebar adjustment would take care of my problem.

"How about three-fourths of an inch?" Conrad asked, loosening the headset with a wrench. Less than an inch hardly seemed significant, but I got back onto the jarring concrete road to try it. My backache disappeared, and I was grateful.

Now I could enjoy Wisconsin's resort country with its woods, lakes, and even an occasional white-tailed deer in a meadow. This was timber country with huge stockpiles of posts in lumber yards, and stacks of firewood alongside homes for next winter. We pedaled by one neat arrangement of cordwood that was bigger than the house.

People in Wisconsin loved to lean out of their car windows and throw questions at us: "Where are you going? Are you in a race? Do you all belong to the same club?" One passenger, probably also a biker, simply said, "Very professional," as he passed cluster two, pedaling along together in a straight line for once.

Another car slowed down next to me. "Was your group in Watertown, South Dakota, a few days ago?"

"Yes."

"We saw you," the young man shouted. I smiled at his exuberance and remembered a lady in the Badlands who had been excited because she had seen us in Portland. They tended to remember all those orange flags and tail patches.

Lakes and woods were our primary environment now, and we listened to insects buzzing like electric appliances, and a bird call similar to a shrill laugh — a loon, perhaps. At a rest break, several of us tried to describe the sound of the constant rustling of leaves in the birch woods.

"The leaves are quaking, fluttering," I said, trying to capture the movement and sound into words.

"It's like rushing water," suggested Mim.

"Or some kind of music," Mary Esch said. "A symphony."

Everyone seemed to be in a congenial mood — helpful and peaceful. But there was turmoil in the world. Besides the fact that Mt. St. Helens erupted again, there were rumblings in the Middle East and war threats among the Arab states. President Carter had declared this the week of U.S. draft registration for nineteen and twenty-year-olds, and that included several of our bikers.

As much as we seemed to be out of touch with world affairs, we had heard about the draft and began re-examining our feelings about war and peace. Ruth had strong Mennonite pacifist views. She argued for the peace cause and often wore a Stop-the-Draft tee-shirt depicting a combat helmet used as a flower planter. Questions abounded as we considered the issues:

"If I register, that doesn't necessarily mean I will be drafted, does it?"

"How can I become a conscientious objector — a C.O.?"

"What happens if I don't register?"

"Should women register, too?"

"How can I register if I'm on this bicycle trip?"

The last question was easy to answer, we learned. Wherever the draft-age young man was on his assigned day of registration, he should go to the local post office and fill out the registry card. Ed and Tony registered in Hertel, Wisconsin; Chip, the next day in Fifield. Ted took their pictures in front of the tiny white-frame post offices.

The picture-taking reminded me of those official photos sent home to Mom from basic training in World War II. We had had one of my brother in his Navy uniform, and a blue star to hang in the window. If Chip, Ed, and Tony were drafted, would they want this picture by the American flag and post office sign? Would their

**Chip registers for the draft in northern Wisconsin.**

moms want such a picture? Did I want a photograph of my son by the Chatsworth Post Office?

Ted and I called home to ask Matt if he had registered. He said he didn't want to be drafted, saw no reason to disrupt his life, give up his job as machinist foreman, to go overseas and kill some other soldiers all because of the gasoline shortage. But he would sign up on Friday, anyway.

I didn't want my son to be trained to kill, but I was relieved that he was abiding by the law, and told him so. Yet I definitely leaned toward pacifism; I agreed with the Mennonite position.

"The U.S. can 'afford' to have only a few pacifists," Ted argued as we lounged at lunch break on our way to Foxfire campground near Woodruff. "If the whole nation believed that way, we would be overrun by stronger nations."

"Aggressors always have to have armies," Ruth was leaning against a huge granite boulder in the center of the grassy plot. She had researched the subject and argued that the U.S. has been an aggressor economically and territorially. Some of the younger Mennonite bikers entered the discussion, too, but were not clear on all the issues.

"I've heard my dad give good arguments against war," one of them said, "but I can't remember them right now." Ruth said that many young people in the peace churches — Mennonites and Quakers — haven't thought through the implications of being a conscientious objector.

"It's a conviction that killing is immoral," she said. "To be a C.O. is to object actively to what conscience will not allow us to do."

"It's impractical," Ted said, sitting up and stretching. "Our country wouldn't last if all the young men were C.O.'s."

"The concept was impractical in Jesus' time, too," Ruth said. "Nobody's really given it a chance." She stood up, shrugged, and put on her helmet and tail patch.

As we resumed biking, I continued the discussion with myself. Many times I had been through the classic argument of "Wouldn't you fight if you or your family were attacked?" The answer was difficult because at first I wanted to say, "Of course, but that's different from bombing Hiroshima." Still I could see that every act of war is just an extension of the self-defense argument.

Yet I had a vision of the peace on earth that God wants for his people. What if all the world's people — *not* the governing heads of state, powerful industry leaders, or generals, but the people who are sent to fight — decided to stand on their convictions that killing was immoral? I was thinking about people in Russia and China and Iran, and everywhere; those who have to put their lives on the line every time a president or king or prime minister declares war. Suppose they would say, "We won't kill." Wouldn't that end war? Probably not; as long as people had their economic self-interest to protect, the fighting would go on. Economics is a merciless ruler.

Rain was one of the tyrants of the road for us bikers. Our first day in Michigan started with light drizzles, plus plenty of trucking traffic, and even a blasting zone to pedal through. A steep hill loomed behind the big orange, diamond-shaped sign identifying the zone. We pedaled up, along with a lane full of cars and trucks. "Go back and wait by the sign," shouted a swarthy construction worker.

"Down the hill?" We all complained about making the climb twice.

"Get down the hill and hurry," he repeated as he waved the other traffic on. "You won't be able to get through before the blast. Now get out of here."

We reached the bottom of the hill in time to hear the dynamite go off and see rocks, rubble, and dust fly up in the air. Coming out from his shelter in the road ditch, the flagman waved us up the hill again, and through the blasting zone. I could look down the ravine where large boulders had been dislodged to prepare for a new bridge. Baseball-sized rocks lay on the side of the road.

Crossing through Michigan's Upper Peninsula, cut off from the rest of the state by water, we were approaching Lake Michigan along a series of bays. Little Bay de Noc, off of Big Bay de Noc, off of Green Bay, which is a bay of Lake Michigan. Finally sighting the shore of Lake Michigan, we decided it looked enough like an ocean to be the Atlantic.

"Let's pretend it is," said Tony as he ran through the misty haze into the water for a quick dip.

"Take our picture," Chip called as he plunged into the cold water. "We'll just say this is Hampton Beach."

"Then we can go home," Tony shouted as he bounded back onto the beach and covered up the Lake Michigan sign. We had already gone over twenty-five hundred miles and I was beginning to get mixed feelings about the trip — anxious for completion but at the same time sad that we were nearing the end. I remembered how I had felt when I first read through the schedule in the Out-Spokin' literature. I practically had tears in my eyes when I came to New England. And soon that would be for real.

Back on the road, the Michigan truck traffic was accelerating. Our portion of the two-lane road was too narrow for a truck alongside a group of bikers. Even when there was ample room, passing trucks created unusual wind currents. I was frightened by the Michigan truck drivers.

Sherm was riding behind me when the call came: "Ditch. Wide load."

"Whoa."

"Are you okay?" Sherm asked as his bike hit my back derailleur.

"I didn't see you there," I answered after I had turned sharply to the right onto the loose gravel on the road's shoulder.

Whoosh. The wide truck and trailer passed by. Although tottering from our slight collision, Sherm and I both managed to keep our bikes upright. I hated to think of Sherm falling on gravel again.

"The biggest scab in the world" is what his friends called his wound. Some of them even took pictures of the bumpy, multi-colored new skin growth that covered one third of his thigh. After two days of resting in the van, on doctor's orders, Sherm had resumed riding. The doctors were now amazed how fast the huge sore was healing. According to Doug's biking magazines, the increased circulation from biking was helping Sherm to get well faster. Now if we could just escape those trucks.

Saturday traffic along the north shore of Lake Michigan included trucks, campers, and boat trailers continually passing us. And we had five more miles of it. My rear-view mirror kept showing me big vehicles overtaking us, thundering toward us, monopolizing the entire environment. We were riding through a forty-mile wide

**Junior has a knee wound cleansed after a fall.**

stretch of land, the peninsula between Lakes Superior and Michigan. On the map, the route looked appealing, but the reality was one of trucks and danger and ditching.

The dangers, our close call with the wide load, and the continuing threat for five more miles began to overwhelm me. Tears came to my eyes as sobs strangled in my throat. I would give anything, I said to myself, if I didn't have to ride these remaining miles.

Yet this was a short biking day for us, only forty-six miles. We would have lunch when we arrived at Naubinway, on the northernmost shore of Lake Michigan. For the evening meal, members of the Mennonite church were arranging a fish fry. We would also be guests at the laundromat, owned by a church member, where we could wash our clothes free of charge and also take hot showers. Sounded like an ideal arrangement.

All these things to look forward to, but I would have given them all up if somehow I could get off this road. I was in no condition to think of high-flown theories of peace on earth or beauty of the countryside or even the thrill of biking cross-country. I felt I was in mortal danger and I wanted out.

I pedaled on, my muscles tensed, awaiting the next air-horn blast, order to ditch, or hulking truck blotting out the view in my mirror. I prayed for deliverance, safety, and strength to endure — at least until Naubinway.

# 17

# Snug Little Island

TALK ABOUT a reluctant bridegroom. When I stepped onto the boat, I may have felt I was eloping, but there was one problem. Ted was almost a block behind me.

With most of the afternoon and evening free, we had walked the several miles from our campground into St. Ignace to look around and have dinner. "If the Mackinac boat is leaving soon," I suggested to Ted, "let's go to the island."

"What for?"

"We can eat dinner there. I love islands. It would be fun." I wanted to do something daring, but Ted was not in the mood.

"The schedule probably wouldn't work out."

"We can check it anyway," I said. "That sign says the terminal is one mile further. Let's walk faster."

"We're going to the island tomorrow with the group. Isn't that enough?"

"Look. This sign says parking for the ferry. I'm going to ask that man."

"We're obviously not there yet."

The man in the parking lot said he thought the ferry docked a few more miles down the lakeshore. St. Ignace basked in the late afternoon sunshine, fresh lake breeze, and temporary respite from frantic tourist traffic. Beckoning signs called our attention to woolens, pasties (an English style meat pie), "olde-tyme" photos, and fudge. Mackinac Island was famous for its fudge, and the candy business floated out in all directions.

"Let's walk faster, Ted. It'd be terrible to miss the boat."

"It probably doesn't run in the evening."

147

"Doesn't that sign say Mackinac Island ferry? And there's a big boat there, too."

"Here's a camera store open, and I've been wanting to buy some film."

Ted turned in at the open door.

"I'll run ahead to the ticket booth and see if we can get on."

"I don't know if I want to go tonight," he called over his shoulder.

"Then I'll go by myself." That man could be quite exasperating, I thought, as I took off with a determined stride up the dock. Why did I always have to push him to do these things? Why did we always have this conflict?

I read the posted schedule: the last boat coming back was at 11:00 P.M. and it took one-half hour to cross the approximately three miles of Lake Huron to the island. "How soon is the boat leaving?" I asked.

"In five minutes," the woman at the ticket counter said.

Perfect. I turned around to see Ted coming out of the camera store. I motioned for him to hurry.

"How many tickets do you want?"

"Two," I said. Surely he would go if I dragged him up the gangplank. Instead, he slowly approached the boarding area and we were the last of only a handful of passengers going to the island on this late afternoon crossing.

But hundreds were coming back, as we could see when we passed a returning ferry; the railings were jammed with people. Ted and I sat in the bow of the ship where cold winds soon demanded the sweaters, windbreakers, and wool hats we had brought along. The sun was still bright, and the air was clear enough to see details on the island after just a few minutes out from shore.

On the island's cliff, a huge, white structure with white columns in front and flags flapping in the breeze caught our attention first. Slanting rays of sun next highlighted a row of large Victorian mansions with gingerbread trim, cupolas, dormers, towers, verandas, gargoyles, and more flagpoles. These houses on the bluffs glowed in rainbow colors like a paint advertisement.

"Aren't you glad you came?" I asked. We were sitting close together for warmth, on the bench in front of the pilot house. I combed Ted's beard with my fingers. I was trying to coax him back into his contented Naubinway mood from the day before. We had stretched out on Lake Michigan's gravel beach in the afternoon sun there, after our laundering and showering were finished. The late-day sunshine was like a blanket on our backs as we lay close together out of the wind. We were sleeping on our own private, deserted island, free from Michigan's threatening trucks at last. I was at peace again with my world, and Ted seemed to be contented as well.

We liked the town of Naubinway. It had a hard-bitten, Maine-seacoast look to it. Even on a sunny summer day, I could sense overshadowing reminders of fierce winters, harsh blizzards, and wind whipping up the entire length of Lake Michigan. Neat but plain houses and yards indicated that the people were frugal and practical.

Church bells rang out at five o'clock, reverberating their tones throughout Naubinway's small settlement, downhill toward the boundless water, and calling Ted and me back to the Mennonite church where we were staying. In a few minutes we walked from the lakeshore to the white, frame building with large, black, gothic lettering on the side: *Jesus is the Answer.* Beneath that proclamation, church members had arranged picnic tables for our feast, and the cooking fire was started.

A heavy iron pot of oil hung on a tripod over the fire. The man in charge of the fish-fry lowered into the hot oil a basket containing fresh whitefish and later, french-cut potatoes. Ted asked him about the fishing in the lake. "Lots of whitefish here," he said. "Our fishing fleet is right up the shore about a mile."

The women of the church, some wearing traditional Mennonite white-lace caps, were setting out casseroles, beans, salads, homemade rolls, and pies. Several members of the Naubinway congregation joined us in the meal as we all sat beneath the giant words: *Jesus is the Answer.* Two of the young men wore fringe beards around clean-shaven faces. Ruth explained to Ted and me that the style was a pacifist protest during the Civil War. "The military then all wore moustaches, but no beards," she said, "so the Mennonites took the opposite approach, a beard but no moustache."

I thought of the Charlie Brown cartoon that takes the opposite approach to *Jesus is the answer.* A comic-strip character carries a sign that says, "What is the question?"

Wasn't that one of the things I wanted to explore on this trip? What are my questions? I guess I could boil things down into one question: How should I live? The answer shone out of the lives of my fellow bikers, people along the way, from my relationship with Ted, and from within myself. Christ shows me the way. Jesus is the answer for the Mennonites in Naubinway, the cross-country bikers, and the Johnsons from Chatsworth.

Although the next day was Sunday and I was interested in attending my first Mennonite service, we had to leave too early for that. This time, Helen routed us away from the lakeshore drive and its truck traffic. We rolled through a misty morning, past isolated countryside and woods.

Leading my cluster, I was enjoying the solitude when two figures emerged from the haze. One was tall, the smaller one seemed to be rolling along. As I approached, I could see he was in a wheelchair being pushed by the other, a younger man.

"Good morning," I said as we met.

The young man nodded, "Hello," but the elderly man in the wheelchair lifted his cane in a salute to us. His eyes glowed with some kind of a tribute as they met mine. Was he saying, "I used to do things like that," or "I'm glad you can," or "Peace be with you"? I didn't know, but I delighted in the contact between biker and "native." Sometimes I saw a person tending a small, backyard vegetable garden and called out, "Nice garden," as I pedaled by. And they looked pleased. In Wisconsin and Minnesota we often saw people at the end of the day resting in their lawn chairs, just watching the traffic. Neither biker nor spectator said anything, but we made contact. Our eyes met and I felt I had communicated with another neighbor along the way.

But I reveled in a lack of traffic, one of the major attractions for me of Mackinac Island. There would be peace from the internal combustion machine on this island, with nothing but horse-drawn vehicles and bicycles. Actually the island maintains one ambulance, fire truck, and public utility truck for emergencies. But that's all. Michigan brags that the island's state highway has never had a motor vehicle accident.

As Ted and I disembarked from the Mackinac Island ferry, we saw a line-up of horsedrawn taxis, racks of bicycles, and bales of hay being unloaded from the boat onto a horse-drawn wagon. The island streets were a throbbing, whirring symphony of bikes — tandems, delivery bikes with large baskets, balloon-tired one-speeds, ten-speeds, and children's bicycles. Near the dock, Mackinac's main street was crowded with cycle rental stores, fudge parlors, and shops.

Ted and I ventured onto side streets where we found historical remnants of the island's frontier days. In 1780, the English had moved an old French garrison from the mainland to this strategic island guarding the Straits of Mackinac. A military stronghold until 1895, Mackinac is now primarily a summer resort, open from May until October. The name was originally Michilimackinac, an Indian word for "Great Turtle."

Walking by old churches and a chapel built of tree bark, we came to Island House, the island's oldest hotel, built in 1848. The multi-storied, white-frame building with columns and verandas was impressive, but it wasn't big enough to be the structure we had seen from the ferry. "Let's look for that tomorrow," Ted suggested as we settled on one of the hotel's verandas overlooking the harbor and main-street bicycle traffic.

I was glad that he was relaxing. We watched the hotel's bell-boy maneuver, by bicycle, a dolly-truck of luggage down the driveway. On the street, shoppers pedaled along behind piles of bags and packages in front baskets, peering around them to check on the traffic. "I understand now why Helen doesn't want us to bring our bikes tomorrow," I said.

"We wouldn't exactly fit in," Ted agreed. We laughed at the thought of one of our clusters whizzing through that scene below, calling out hazards, signaling stops, and thoroughly confusing the island cyclists.

"I wish we could spend the night here," Ted said.

"Could we?"

"We don't even have a toothbrush with us."

"We could buy one and share it."

But how could we let Helen know where we were? She would worry about us all night if we didn't show up.

We gave up the idea of staying, but I felt that Ted was getting into the ways of the island. When we came back again the next morning with the rest of the bikers, we felt as though we were coming home. This time we climbed the hill to reach the huge, columned landmark on the cliff, the Grand Hotel itself, built ninety-eight years ago.

"The largest porch in the world" is how the hotel describes its veranda. When you stand at one end, you can almost imagine two lanes of traffic coming down the astro-turf carpet. Red geraniums, the hotel's logo, cascade from flowerboxes alternating with huge white columns on your right, and three rows of hotel windows disappear into infinity on your left.

Down a few steps, beneath the four gigantic American flags, horsedrawn taxis regularly discharge passengers. Across the entry road are gardens, and further down the cliff, two swimming pools. We collapsed into two empty chaise lounges. Our view stretched across the Straits to St. Ignace, and we could see our campground near the bend of shore, and the five-mile Mackinaw Suspension Bridge we would be crossing the next day.

Sitting on the porch was free, but the cheapest accommodations in the hotel were $90 per person per night, meals included. House rules decreed that women wear skirts after 5:00 P.M. and men wear jackets and ties. What would the roomclerk have done with us the night before if we had tried to check in wearing our grubby sweaters and windbreakers, and carrying no luggage? And how would we have felt when presented with the bill?

"Ted, do you ever want to come back here and stay at the Grand Hotel?"

"Sure. When should we?"

"How about our fiftieth anniversary? We could visit several islands — Mackinac, Royal Isle, Catalina —"

"Sounds good."

"I've got a better idea. We could visit famous old lodges, like the one at Old Faithful. I still want to see Old Faithful, you know."

"Why not? Anything seems possible now," Ted said, soaking up the island's atmosphere.

As we headed back to our group's meeting place at the harbor park, I spotted the Topside Bookstore between one last fudge parlor and souvenir shop. I decided to make a quick stop, took the narrow steps up to the store two at a time, and greeted a Dickens-like man sitting at the cash register.

"I'm looking for a book," I stated, breathless from the climb and the knowledge that we had fifteen minutes before our group would catch the ferry. "Would you believe it, I can't even remember the title now."

"As soon as you calm down," he said, peering at me critically over his half-glasses, "you'll probably think of it."

Was I that uptight? After this lovely, leisurely day, was I still wound up? Was I pushing again? I purposefully slowed down and began to collect my thoughts, trying to think of that book title.

Of course, I recalled, the book was Annie Dillard's *Pilgrim at Tinker Creek*, the only book besides my Bible that I had brought along. I was reading Annie Dillard for the third time because I enjoyed her spiritual descriptions of nature and living interpretations of the gospel. I had lent it to Barbara Haya during a morning quiet time, and I wanted to buy her one now.

The little man peered around the bookshelf at me. "How are you doing?"

"I thought of the book," I said, talking and breathing slowly. He helped me find the Dillard book, had me sign a special card — perhaps reserved for "hyper" types who cool down under his influence — and then presented me with the pen. I took his picture as part of the exchange and wished I could be a regular patron of the bookstore.

I wanted to be part of an island literary group that congregated, I imagined, around this bookstore. It would be a leisurely paced group, I was sure, who bicycled about carrying a favorite tome in their bike baskets, and pausing to read at one of the cliff view-points or the Grand Hotel veranda. That gave me an idea. I ran outside and shouted across the park to my husband, "Ted, do we have to leave the island now?"

Ted was strongly under the island's influence. "No," he said, "let's catch a later ferry."

We walked to the dock with our fellow bikers and saw them off, waving and calling, "Write to us. We'll see you in a year," and other silly things. Then we went to the deli and bought bean salad, cheese, yogurt, grapes, and bread. Ted and I picnicked in the last rays of sunshine on the harbor park lawn. We watched the boats, people, horses, and bicycles. I was no longer a slave to anybody's schedule. Thank you, Mr. Topside Bookstore.

# 18

# A Broken Bone

**M**ARV ESCH was going home. But only for one night, and he was bringing twenty-eight bikers with him. "Hey, Mom, can my friends stay overnight?"

The 175-acre Esch farm in Fairview, Michigan, was an official, scheduled stop on our route. As we all shared with Marv's family and friends about our trip, none of us could foresee that Marv would soon be relegated to riding in the van before he even left his home state. Marv, the happy, bubbly, energetic, praise-the-Lord, super-pedaler, who wrote most of the verses to "We Won't Stop Biking Until Hampton Beach," would have to stop.

His mother, Velma, was a second-grade teacher and mother of seven. She had the same kind of enthusiasm and friendliness as her son Marv, as she made her twenty-eight guests comfortable. She insisted that Ted and I sleep on their fold-out sofa — with pillows, even. Marv's dad, Ira, took Ted and me on a farm tour that included an immaculate hog barn, complete with piped in music.

"Classical music keeps them more docile," he explained as we heard a violin concerto floating over the heads of the big, bristling mother sows and piglets. Ted's farm background always seemed to surface when he talked to farmers on our trip; he knew the "language."

Fellow Mennonites in the Fairview area brought in extra food to add to an already abounding feast. We left the next day with pleasant memories, plus cookies that weren't consumed the night before, and several jars of fresh milk.

Somehow mid-Michigan even smelled different; it reminded me of burnt marshmallows, charcoal, diesel fuel, and asphalt. We stopped at a filling station near Kawkawlin for a break and sat among some broken concrete and weeds, away from the gas pumps and traffic. A tourist asked us about the trip.

"I used to bike," said the man, whom I judged to be about my age. "I did 190 miles once in 20 hours."

"That's great," I said. "Why don't you ride anymore?"

"My doctor won't let me." He turned away. I felt sorry for him and happy for Ted and me. We were blessed, I knew, to still have knees that worked — even if they hurt sometimes — and good lungs and hearts that could do the job. I was grateful for our good health and became more determined to stay that way. Diet, exercise, peace with God and neighbor and self. I was working out these things as I pedaled along.

That night we were staying at the Bay City South Baptist Church. Todd's father, who was making sales calls in the area, was going to join us, and I looked forward to meeting him. Visiting us also were Kirk's family from Elkhart, Indiana.

Kirk's parents had been coordinators on the first Out-Spokin' trip in 1969, driving a camper and forty-foot trailer. As we stood in the church parking lot, unloading the van, we heard about that first trip. Kirk's mother said she had cooked for the 40 bikers and also taken care of her four children. I couldn't imagine a cross-country trip with forty cyclists and four little kids.

"I was only six then," Kirk recalled, "but I knew I would take the trip when I was old enough."

"The bikers were all guys," Kirk's mother continued, "and they averaged 160 miles a day. One day on the plains they did 220 miles."

Most of us unloading duffels stopped to listen; no one could believe these stories. How different it must have been then! We had just finished ninety miles and were exhausted.

After Kirk's family went out to dinner, I still thought about that first trip and wondered how the Out-Spokin' bikers of 1969 had trained for their tour. Did they have slow bikers, accidents, or any of the troubles we were encountering? Was there a Junior among those forty? Obviously, there weren't any Barbies or Michelles, or Babs, for that matter.

We were just settling into the spacious three-story urban church when Todd's father arrived. Ted and I met him in the hallway. "I'm combining a business trip with a visit with my son," explained the short, young-looking man, whose first name was Ted, also. He told my Ted that he could never take time off from his sales work to go on a bicycle trip like this, but would like to.

"Do you think Todd's enjoying the trip?" I asked. I didn't want to pry but it seemed like a natural question. Todd was off, getting cleaned up to go out to dinner, and we could talk freely.

"Yes, I do," he said. "And I've seen quite a change in him. He seems more grown-up and responsible now. He talks more. When he calls home on the phone now, he just talks and talks and tells us all the things that are happening. He never used to have anything to say to me or his mother."

I knew how that was. Our conversations with our son were usually, "How are you?" "Fine." "What's new?" "Nothing." I was glad Todd was talking to his parents, but I wondered if he really told them everything that was going on.

"You know he's had trouble in school," Todd's father continued, "and he's had to have some counseling because he just doesn't like regulations."

I remained silent. I didn't feel it was my place to tell him about Todd's problems with group rules — how he ran away or broke the hinge on the schoolhouse door. I hoped Helen would. Yet she may have been struggling with doubts, guilts and angers, too, just as the rest of us were. After all, she had told me that she would do things differently if she had the chance again. "Sometimes I don't know what it all means," she said. "A Christian community working together. I don't know how to put it all together in my mind."

Perhaps I was expecting too much of our coordinator. Maybe it wasn't even necessary to tell Todd's father. Perhaps these episodes would be secrets for now, to be divulged by Todd months, or perhaps years later. When our daughter Judy was going to college in Iowa, we didn't hear about any of her escapades until her letters reached us much later. How could we worry about her hitchhiking to a concert when it occurred the month before? Or taking part in a student demonstration that disintegrated into rock-throwing? That was history. We just put our trust in the Lord and in Judy's growing judgment. Perhaps Todd was over his problems now.

"The good thing about this trip," Todd's father was saying, "is that there is a goal to strive for. That's its uniqueness. Todd will probably look back on this experience, after it's all over, and think it was one of the greatest times of his life."

"That could be true," I admitted.

"You know, I've come up with a definition for happiness, after thinking about it for a long time." Todd's dad had a direct, friendly, but intense manner. "Happiness is anticipation or reflection, never the present. You're either looking forward to something, or back at it."

"I like to think that we only have the present," I argued, but I decided to think about his idea while biking the next day. I would also try to piece together what I knew about Todd, his behavior on the trip so far, and his father's personality. He was a man of many talents: he had told us about a rhyming dictionary he was compiling, and his tailoring and dressmaking ability. He said he had made the smart-looking duffel Todd had brought and, more surprising to me, the formal prom dresses for his three daughters.

He was also a success in his work, but he didn't believe in happiness in the present. That idea bothered me. I believe that God is with me right now. If I spend too much time thinking about the past or future, I'll never experience the present moment, which is my reality, the life I'm living, the world in which I exist.

At the Esch home, I had seen wooden plaques that Velma was preparing for a large fund-raising sale for Mennonite relief work. I bought the one that said, "I am not afraid of tomorrow, for I have seen yesterday and I love today." How did that fit with Todd's father's idea? Didn't that take his concept one step further and help us to understand that we can bask in God's love now, and praise the Lord for this very instant?

At any rate, I "loved" the next evening in Imlay City, where we relaxed on a shady lawn beside the swimming pool at Phil and Ruth Rittger's country estate. Members from their Mennonite church brought in a generous feast for us. We savored it all, including a birthday cake for Junior's 18th. "Some party for you, Junior," I remarked.

"Nothing but the best." He looked happy when all those people, about sixty of us, sang to him. Then we gathered together for another program, more formalized than our sharing in South Dakota. Each of us this time gave one particular bit of information, and I found it to be a nostalgic review of our trip.

Ed started: "We've had 135 flats so far; forty tires have been replaced. Ted calculated that, by the end of the trip, our pedals will have made 1.8 million revolutions."

Chip admitted that living out of a duffle bag had taught him organization. "It's tough not having Mom around," he said. But I had seen him and the others learning to cope.

"Being on this trip has made me realize how much I love my family," Todd said. "Now that I've been away I know how much they do to help me." Todd's father, still visiting with us each evening, was sitting at the edge of the group. He looked very pleased with his son. I hoped that the trip would have a happy ending for Todd and his father. I decided it didn't matter if Helen had the conference with him or not.

Junior, who claimed earlier he couldn't think of anything to say, told the group he was inspired by the beauty of the Badlands. "It's amazing what God can do," he said, "with a little dirt, rock, and water." We laughed, but I was seeing a new side of Junior. All along, I had thought he didn't look at the scenery. Mountains were only impassable barriers to him. But the Badlands had touched him.

Cluster three closed the program with their original song, "We Won't Stop Biking Until Hampton Beach." Marv Esch was singing with the group as they all waved their safety flags to punctuate the beat. No one suspected then what was in store for Marv.

We were leaving Michigan's hospitality, trucks, and bad pavement the next day for Ontario, Canada. My cluster was waiting at a fork in the road outside of Port Huron to flag the corner for cluster three, when a driver stopped to tell us there had been an accident in the group behind us.

Who was it? Once again we waited and worried and wondered, and prayed. At our next break, Marv's wrist was swollen. He was hurting. He said his front wheel had struck the edge of the road as he turned to avoid a bumpy shoulder. He was dumped onto the pavement, landing with all his weight on his right hand. In shock at first, he was helped by people who lived near the accident site.

They came out and took the injured rider, and his bike, in their truck to our rest stop.

Helen told Marv they would get to a doctor in Canada. "I'll just store your bike in the trailer for now," she said as Marv climbed into the van. I felt sorry for him. How quickly our dreams can be smashed.

Crossing the border could take minutes, or hours, Helen warned the group: "It all depends upon the mood of the officials and our deportment." We were going over the St. Clair River into Sarnia, Ontario. The officials prohibited us from riding our bicycles across the border bridge so we pushed the bikes instead, still keeping pace with the slow-moving traffic. Our interrogation went without incident.

This was a totally new experience for many of the young bikers.

They spotted the distinct Canadian style in colorful paper money, with its touches of blue, yellow, and orange; the little crowns on Canadian highway signs, and bright red mailboxes. We noticed that Canadians put their names in large white letters on their red barns and planted formal rows of trees to line driveways and roads. Red and white maple-leaf Canadian flags waved at us from farmyards and hotels. We glided past tobacco sheds, a silver fox farm, and two Amish children on a horse-drawn wagon. I slowed down for a few minutes to hear harmonica music floating out from a tiny roadside vegetable stand. The beauty of it all filled me with appreciation.

Once again, however, the reality of our situation hit me. Our Canadian tour that day would be a grueling 110 miles — endless miles for Marv, traveling in the van with his injured wrist, waiting to see a doctor.

We all must have sounded like unappreciative ingrates when we arrived at our London, Ontario, campground — hot, tired, having been lost for a while, and angry at clusters who didn't mark certain turns. Accusations were thrown out and returned by overwrought bikers.

"Why didn't you wait for us?"
"You forgot to flag."

"Didn't you notice that we were missing?"

"It's all your fault."

"You don't care about the rest of the group."

"How could you be so thoughtless?"

Audience to our charges and countercharges were twenty members of the local Mennonite church who had been waiting for our arrival, trying to keep dinner hot, and their small children away from the tempting array of food. I hoped they weren't offended by our behavior, but I was too tired to say anything conciliatory.

Our welcoming group seemed like a unique group of helpful people. Some of the men had even set up our tents while they were waiting for us, and one woman offered to go with Helen and Marv to the hospital.

The rest of us forgot our spat as we enjoyed the satisfying meal the group provided. Huddled on the lawn after dinner, we swatted mosquitoes and tried to share, through our fatigue, what it was like to be a cross-country biker on August 1, 1980 in London, Ontario. We weren't as talkative as we had been at the Rittgers', but repeated some of the same information. When we ran out of comments, we said good-night and thanks, and limped off to our tents.

Earlier, as we had ridden into town around 7:00 P.M., a young child had asked us why we were biking. Our cluster had been stopped at a traffic light by a park where several children climbed the jungle gym. "Why are you biking?" was the question thrown out by a dark-haired girl in pigtails.

"Oh, they don't answer", she said to her playmates.

How can you avoid a comment such as that? I had to reply. "We're biking for fun," I said as the traffic light changed and we went on.

Incredible that I should have said that, I thought now. I zipped up our tent and sank down on the sleeping bag beside Ted. Yet, in a strange way, I still agreed with my answer. It was fun; I knew that I could look back and laugh at us. Maybe this was another facet of Todd's father's philosophy.

Helen could laugh the next morning. "We know each other well

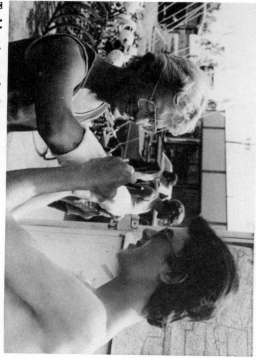

**Todd autographs Marv's cast.**

enough now to let it all hang out," she said. "We've become a family when we can argue like we did last night and still stay together."

But Marv wasn't laughing. His right arm was in a cast from his wrist nearly to his elbow. And eleven days were left before the end of our trip.

"I don't know how I'm going to ride my bike," he said, trying to wiggle his immobile fingers, "but I know I'm not going home before Hampton Beach."

# 19

# Fear of Dying

**W**HEN I HEARD that a cyclist had been hit, I instantly thought it was Ted. Just as when the phone rings in the middle of the night, I always assume it is bad news.

It started out as a routine stop for cluster two. Junior had a broken spoke after we had pedaled only about a mile from Don and Ellen Frey's country home outside of Akron, New York. Our stay there had been another delightful overnight mini-holiday. Now a car braked to a stop on the shoulder behind us. The driver, carrying a walkie-talkie, was out of his vehicle in an instant. "Someone hurt?" he asked.

"No," Doug answered. "We've just got a broken spoke."

"I heard on the CB that a cyclist had been hit and assumed you were the group," the man said.

We looked up the road toward the crest of the hill, about a mile away. The lights of an emergency vehicle were flashing. "That must be it," the man said, driving off and leaving us with our questions.

"Cluster four is right ahead of us," I said. If it were cluster four, could it be Ted? Or Kirk? I glanced at Barbie. We were all staring at those lights.

But the victim could be in any cluster, I knew. The others would have stopped to help, so it could be anyone. Except cluster two; we were last today.

"I don't think we want to add to the confusion," Doug said. "We'd better wait here."

I didn't want to wait, but I took off my helmet and hung it over my bike seat, getting as comfortable as I could for the long wait. I

163

watched the hypnotic lights — on again, off again. A cyclist had been hit, I repeated to myself. Why couldn't I leave my cluster for once and go up there and find out who it was? In my mind, I was already a widow. Would I be coming back from this trip with a body in a coffin instead of a husband sitting at my side? I wanted to know now.

"Let's pray," Doug said. We huddled together on the shoulder of the road. We were all alone. No traffic was going by. Heads bowed, eyes closed, we each added to the prayer. "Dear God," Doug began, "we just don't know what is happening ahead of us on the road. We pray that you will be with those who are hurting and sustain us in this trial."

"We don't understand why these things have to happen, Lord," Mike prayed, "but help us through it."

"Show us how we can help in any way," I added.

"Thy will be done."

Now we just stood there, waiting, lost in our own thoughts and prayers. Waiting, not knowing, was difficult, but I also hated to approach that scene up ahead. I wanted to know, yet I didn't want to know. Ted was a careful rider, that I was sure of. He had never had a serious cycling accident, so maybe it wasn't him after all. But anything could happen, even on a quiet country road.

I leaned against my bike now, still staring at those flashing emergency lights ahead, and recalled how muddy the bikes had been after a Canadian rain in Ontario two days before. We had pedaled through a drenching downpour, our twelfth day of rain on the trip. I remembered how happy Ted and I were to arrive finally at Wainfleet's Church of the Brethren.

We set up house in the pastor's dressing room, next to the chancel of a large sanctuary. After sleeping in the Drummond, Montana, confessional room, we had become less timid about our quarters.

I washed out some of our mud-splotched clothes and hung them about the open window. Ted rolled out our sleeping bags on the carpet and put my typewriter on a little work table. We felt right at home.

Just before lights-out time, with Ted lying on the sleeping bags in his pajamas and me at the typewriter, the door suddenly opened. It was the minister of the church. He glanced about at the strange transformation his room had undergone. "I don't believe it," he said.

"Oh, we'll have it all back the way it was," Ted assured him, sitting up halfway and reaching for his glasses. "In plenty of time for tomorrow's service, too."

"We're the only married couple, you know," I added. "That's why we're in this room." We seemed to be talking faster than usual, talking ourselves out of an eviction.

"We really appreciate your generosity," I continued, "in letting us use your church."

"It's all right." The minister laughed, still standing at the doorway, one hand gripping the doorknob as we smiled and nodded at him. "I just thought I had forgotten to turn off the light. That's the reason I opened the door. Fine, fine. Have a good night's rest." He closed the door and we sighed in relief. From where the minister had been standing, he couldn't see the window with the wet wash.

It rained all night, anyway, so the clothes didn't even get a chance to dry. But the next morning cleared and we were off to Niagara. We had been given a free half-day to see the falls. This was a sight we would not want to miss. Ted and I hung up the laundry again at Falls View Church in Niagara Falls, Ontario.

We walked from there to the Niagara River, toward the roar of the falls, trying to imagine the excitement and fear of explorers approaching the drop-off in a boat.

With hundreds more pedestrians, we walked through Niagara mist and tourist traffic. At least half of the crowd were foreigners: Indian ladies in saris, Japanese sightseers with their cameras, and people speaking languages we couldn't recognize. We found a nearly deserted terrace above the main viewing plazas, just right for us to inhale the mystique of Niagara. We could view both Canadian and American cascades; the multi-colored, swarming crowd of humanity in the bright sunshine; Maid o' the Mist boats on the river below straining against the force of the falls; and a line of tourists in yellow slickers climbing trails to the caves on the American side. The scene reminded me of a cartoonist's map depicting all the tourist sights available.

On our terrace we felt remote from these crowds. Leaning against a window ledge of the tourist center, we waited as shade inched its way toward an empty bench facing the panoramic scene below. We were in no hurry. We would move when the shade reached the bench. I loved being relaxed and outside of schedules and rules. We could simply enjoy ourselves, the drama of the waterfall, and the constant kaleidoscope of the crowds of people below.

We felt at peace with the present moment. We weren't planning our next activity or reflecting back on the past. We seemed to be complete in each other's company, more than I could recall on any other vacation. Had the trip brought us closer together? Was it for the best after all that I had talked Ted into going on the trip? Was it good for both of us? I think I learned to appreciate Ted's company more than ever. We realized that we could enjoy a retirement life of traveling for entire summers, or winters, seeking new experiences and vistas. That knowledge opened up our future.

Was I more appreciative of God's beauty because of the trip? I had seen Niagara when I was a child, but now I had bicycled thirty-three hundred miles to get there. That made a difference. I was changed; I felt an awe that I hadn't felt as a child. I could hardly believe the force and power of Niagara. I admired the beauty and was thankful that I could look at this scene, inhale its essence, store it in my memory, compare it with other natural wonders, and feel closer to the Creator by appreciation of His creation. Yes, I think I could now say that the Lord sent us on this trip.

I thought back on these happy moments as I stood on the side of the road in western New York state, waiting to learn who had been hit in the accident up the road. We couldn't bicycle up there because Junior had a broken spoke. We waited for Conrad.

I looked at my clustermates, my close companions for all these miles. Junior was lighter in weight but heavier in confidence, and Barbie had grown in maturity over the weeks.

I remembered the day in Canada when Barbie had hyperventilated and I had been frightened by her dilemma. When she had started gasping for air, I kept remembering how I had been pushing her. Was she dramatizing her struggle to keep up just to get attention? Or was she looking for sympathy?

Hill after hill, I could hear Barbie panting behind me as we reached the crest. She was taking the air by huge gulps and making vomiting sounds. "Aug-gh-gh-gh."

"Are you all right?" I turned my head to look at her.

"Have to stop." With each breath, she gagged.

The whole group braked to a stop to gather around Barbie. Her face was flushed; her blue eyes widened as she struggled for air. Everyone was giving instructions, but Doug took charge. He rubbed her back until she began to calm down. The gagging sound stopped. Then she laughed.

I would have to let Barbie go at her own speed; I couldn't push her anymore. As a sixteen-year-old, Barbie had gumption to come on this trip alone. She was a person with enthusiasm, good humor, and independent spirit, and a bright future. I would like to bicycle with her again.

In fact, I had recently issued a blanket invitation to bicycle with any member of our group when they reached their fiftieth birthday— if they were still biking! Naturally, I intended to be biking, even though I would be somewhere between the age of seventy-six and eighty-six.

And Ted, too? My thoughts brought me back to the accident ahead. I wanted to know who had been hurt. I couldn't stand it any longer. I glanced at Sherm, sitting at the side of the road, head down on his knee. What was he thinking — that the victim was his friend, Linda? Sherm's injury had caused him a lot of suffering, but he had persevered and was almost healed now. He was a sensitive person, I felt, and reflective. I sensed that the trip had affected him deeply and had given him confidence and a feeling of accomplish-ment. "I've grown," he had said. "I don't really know how or in what areas of life, but I've changed."

I looked at Doug next. "Let's start walking," he suggested. Maybe he saw how we were all being affected. "It might be better than waiting here."

I agreed, although my legs seemed unable to support me as I

pushed my bike. I was weak just at the thought of the accident ahead. After we started walking we heard Conrad's motorcycle coming from behind us.

"What now, Junior?" he cheerily called out.

Doug pointed out the lights flashing ahead and told Conrad what the man with the walkie-talkie had said. Conrad roared on by, but was soon coming back to us. "Not one of our group," he called. "I thought it was Ted at first."

My heart skipped a beat.

Conrad went on: "The guy lying on the road had sandy-gray hair. But when I looked at the bike he had been riding, I knew it wasn't ours."

So it wasn't Ted. It wasn't Kirk. It wasn't Linda. Not one of us. We had escaped. We were all safe, at least for now. Prayers of thanks flooded my head. Tears of relief rolled down my cheeks.

But what about the victim, I wondered. The tears of his loved ones would be different from our tears of joy.

# 20

# Pilgrims Find the Way

I HAVE ALWAYS liked graduations. They are emotional events for me, comparable to weddings, funerals, and baptisms. I get choked up just seeing a line of chairs in a schoolyard at graduation time. The concept of an ending and a new beginning excites me.

Hampton Beach, New Hampshire, was going to be our graduation. Wheeling into that beach city, seeing the Atlantic Ocean, dipping our front wheels into the waves, picking up handfuls of sand to fling in the air, and praising God for our safe deliverance. That would be our graduation. But was everyone going to be there?

Could Todd pass his "finals"? Would Marv finally get his chance to bicycle again with the group, to pedal at least that last mile? Would my own husband be in that final procession to the beach?

As Ted resolutely marched to the bicycle store during our break in Brattleboro, Vermont, I seriously began to doubt it. I had been through all this before in West Yellowstone. How could this be happening again so near the end? We were within sight of the finish line.

Several days before Ted's threatened mutiny, we had witnessed Todd's revenge, his reply to those who teased, bugged, bedeviled, belittled, and thwarted him. While still in New York, staying at the Community Center in Oneida, Conrad had barred Todd from the breakfast line. I was surprised to see our staff mechanic standing between Todd and the buffet table. Conrad was obviously blocking the way.

What was going on, I wondered. They both stood there like statues, neither one budging. The rest of us filed past them and loaded up our plates and bowls. A power struggle was going on, I thought, like Helen and Todd and the water bottle. Another personality clash for Todd.

When I waited in line for seconds, and Todd and Conrad were still there, I asked Mike about the situation. "Todd wouldn't move his sleeping bag last night," Mike explained.

That didn't make a whole lot of sense to me. I had heard the men's sleeping quarters were crowded because of a pool table in the center of the room, but what did that have to do with breakfast?

"Some of the guys were crammed together tightly," Mike continued, "and Todd was asked to line up his sleeping bag so there would be more room for the others to stretch out. He refused to move."

Conrad, the only staff member present at the time, Mike said, had given a no-breakfast ultimatum to Todd. But he remained unmoved.

Todd's father had told us he didn't like to take orders. This was a clear-cut example. But what possible difference could it make to Todd whether his sleeping bag was moved slightly one way or the other? Something inside of Todd was making him fight for every inch of his territorial rights, real and imaginary. In this case, he won his right to keep his sleeping bag in place, and went without breakfast as the price.

Two days later in Hoosick Falls, New York, Todd had another victory — not over Conrad, but Ed, who was another symbol of harassment for Todd.

We all had double rooms in the two-story dorm of a private school in Hoosick Falls. The guys were on the second floor, and those who dozed off first were at a disadvantage. Todd was among them.

End-of-the-trip pranks were rampant as graduation fever took hold. "Night raiders," armed with aerosol spray cans of shaving cream, roamed the halls decorating their sleeping prey. Ted and I were safe downstairs in the Fireside Room.

The next morning while Ted and I cleaned the room where we had slept, we could hear bikers waiting in the breakfast line below our window. Daniel was complaining about the mess the shaving cream had made in his beard.

"You're lucky they didn't shave it off," said Mike, who was "creamed" on his neck, shoulders, and back.

As we listened to the comments, Ted and I finished rearranging furniture and picked up scraps of paper from the floor. "Hey, what happened to the trash bucket?" Ted asked.

"Don't know. Use the one in the hall."

Just as we joined the breakfast line, Ed, with hair combed and wearing clean clothes, strolled out the front door of the dorm. A flood of water landed on his head.

"Ohhhh." All the bikers in line stopped their cereal-serving and juice-pouring to look up at the dorm's second story.

"There's our bucket," I said, seeing Todd at the window above the entrance. He held the empty bucket high in triumph. "Right on target, Ed," Todd crowed. "That's for all that shaving cream mess."

"Amen," added Daniel from the breakfast line.

"Right on," Mike laughed.

Shaking water out of his eyes, Ed was stunned. The "wimp" had struck back. I wanted to believe that Todd's bucket of water washed away more than the shaving-cream resentment. The water cleared out a seven-week accumulation of hurts, real and imagined, from snubs to indifference, to punishments of no-water, no-breakfast, and on and on.

Todd had spoken with that bucket of water. I hoped he felt cleansed, forgiven, and ready to start a new day.

Our new day, after this eventful breakfast in New York, called for lunch in Vermont and dinner in New Hampshire. Most of our scheduled seventy-six miles climbed through the Green Mountains of Vermont. The hilly terrain ruled out Marv's chance to try biking again. Despite his cast, he had been practicing biking at breaks and lunchtime. Conrad had switched the brake levers for him so his good left hand could operate the rear wheel brake, which needed the most pressure for a safe stop.

But every day that Marv was ready to pedal off with his cluster,

Helen convinced him that the rain, or pavement, or hills, or long mileage might give him problems. "Tomorrow," she would suggest. She was afraid he might fall again. Bicycling could be dangerous enough even under the best conditions. We had heard that the accident victim in Akron, New York, was still hospitalized with a severe concussion and optic muscle damage.

Helen thought the mountain route would not be Marv's best reintroduction to biking. The hilly terrain of the Green Mountains was also a challenge for Michelle. As she slowed down, Ted's exasperation went up — again.

Too bad, I thought. The weather was perfect, and we were cycling smooth roller-coaster roads, through forest and quaint little towns in the vales such as Bennington. This valley town, presided over by a miniature "Washington monument" for General Burgoyne, was in the midst of a horse show when we went through. Participants in formal riding clothes mingled with spectators gathered around a striped awning tent.

Vermont is one of the few states that forbids billboards. The roadways are pure poetry. Cumulus clouds floated above mountain peaks, and the air was fresh. But Ted said Michelle hardly lifted her head as she crept up the hills at the same speed she had used in Oregon. She told him she was exhausted from the 106-mile trek through humid New York the day before. Ted encouraged her to ride faster, as he led the cluster at his regular swift pace.

But Conrad, riding with them that day, told Ted to slow down. That reprimand did it. "Conrad's acting like a policeman, or some kind of Cub Scout leader," Ted complained to me at our break at Wilmington. The town was clogged with antique-shopping tourists and art patrons. A juggler on the sidewalk entertained the slow-moving traffic.

But Ted couldn't enjoy Wilmington; I had never seen him this angry before. I sympathized with him, but was mystified, once again, at the slow pace and inability of some of our riders to bike up the mountains. After all, we were practically at the end of our ride, I thought. Surely an Out-Spokin' "graduate" could climb the Green Mountains.

"It's mental," Ted said. "They get psyched by the idea of a mountain, shift down into first gear, and go as slow as they can.

They know we all have to stay with them; there's no incentive or motivation. Why should they exert themselves?"

When we reached the summit of Prospect Mountain, a ski area in the winter, Ted was fuming. Helen suggested that cluster four have a "therapy" session to consider Ted's complaints. His cluster was coming apart at the seams. "You need to talk it out," she told Ted.

The six of them stood in a circle on the mountaintop parking lot. I watched from a distance as the other bikers snacked, rested and looked at the view.

Ted told me he had argued his point of keeping a steady pace as the easiest way to climb a mountain. Ruth had tried to be mediator, while Chip sided with Ted. "I've always wanted to ride faster," he said.

Kirk said he didn't care to be rushed. Michelle was quiet and finally left the group to sit on a boulder at the edge of the pavement. She rarely spoke in any group gatherings and hardly ever raised her voice above a whisper. I had probably had only two or three conversations with her the whole trip.

"We have to support the group as a whole," Conrad repeated at the therapy session. "You'll have to hold back your speed, Ted, and help Michelle along."

"I've had it," Ted said as he joined me under the "Ski Prospect" sign. "Our next break is in Brattleboro and I'm going to the bike store."

We had a thirty-minute break in Brattleboro to look around, buy souvenirs, or, in our case, walk to the cyclery six blocks away. The store stocked all the equipment Ted needed — ten-speed bikes, panniers, water bottles, tool kits, and pumps. I was numb, not believing that this was really happening.

"Can I help you?" The sales clerk approached us. Ted fingered bike bags lovingly as he asked if the store accepted his charge card. For approximately $400, Ted could sail through the two-day ride to Hampton Beach at his own speed. I checked my watch; in ten minutes my cluster, lead group for the day, was due to hit the road. Ted's group didn't leave until later. But he would still have to make a quick decision, hurry back to the van to dig out his duffle and sleeping bag, and lug them back to the store to complete his purchases. I noted the deep furrow between his eyebrows as he frowned at the Peugeot, spun the wheels, and checked the brakes. "I have to go back," I said. "You stay and decide. It's completely up to you." I kissed him goodbye and fought back the tears welling up in my eyes.

As I hurried along the streets of Brattleboro, back to our bikes and the van, I thought only of my husband in the bike store. Close to release from his frustrations, he faced a difficult decision. After all, he had a perfectly good bike at home; and $400 for two days? Would each day be worth $200? A steep price, but he would get the rest of Vermont and New Hampshire for it.

These states could come alive for him; he could skim over the crest of hills for panoramic views without dragging reluctant bikers with him. There would be time to explore villages and to stop when we wanted to, at a vegetarian restaurant or art shop.

But wait! I was getting carried away. What was this "we"? I had already decided to stay with the group because I didn't want to carry my own gear.

As my cluster put on helmets and tail patches to lead off again, I didn't tell them what was going on in the Brattleboro bike store. But Ted had not arrived back at the van by the time we pedaled out of town.

If I had learned anything about myself on this trip, it was that I was a finisher. I made my plans carefully, prepared for the event, prayed my way through, and finished. I also learned what a marvelous instrument God has given us in the human body, what things it can do if taken care of and encouraged.

Our Christian community on wheels had taught me how many little ways I could help other people, and let them help me. The opportunities were everywhere, surrounding me; I didn't have to go cross-country to find people who needed my help. I hoped to come home a better servant to others.

Now I wanted to help Ted, but he was on his own. I worried about him taking off, leaving the group, going away disgruntled, unhappy, disappointed, and frustrated. I had talked him into going on this trip. I got us into it. I had been so sure everything would work out okay. Evidently Ted didn't agree.

Yet, during our group evaluation session, Ted had spoken positively about the trip. He had singled out his birthday celebration in Wisconsin as the high point for him. Early in the trip, he had said to me, "Don't even mention my birthday."

But every time Junior had talked about his own birthday, coming up on July 31, I reminded the group that Ted's was just the week before on the 23rd. Helen and Peg knew that Ted didn't eat cake but loved homemade pies. So, at the Calvary Covenant Church in Grantsburg, Wisconsin, several of the women bikers secretly baked pies for Ted's birthday dinner the next night.

"Apple pie? For me?" Ted was thrilled. He was also served a special birthday breakfast of homemade granola, and a fruit-salad lunch complete with a slice of melon with candles stuck into it. Ted was touched by the love and attention showered on him. "I thought you didn't want us to remember your birthday," I had reminded him.

"You can't believe everything I say," he answered.

What about now? Could I believe that he was going to purchase a bike and strike out on his own?

We had crossed the state line after Brattleboro, heading for a campground in Keene, New Hampshire. When we arrived, I anxiously awaited the appearance of cluster four. And there was Ted, leading the way with Michelle a few feet behind him, and all the rest. Everyone present and accounted for.

"I decided it wasn't worth it," Ted answered my questioning look. As soon as he lined up his bike I gave him a welcoming hug.

"Now we can pedal into Hampton Beach together," I said.

That final day was on everyone else's mind, too. Ed and Chip turned their energies to planning one last good time. I heard them talk about racing that last mile to the sea. "We can forget about clusters and all that staying together and single file stuff," Ed said. "We'll just get a group together and go for it, flat-out."

"What could Helen do?" Chip asked.

"It's the last day."

"And we'll decorate our bikes with crepe paper and American flags."

Maybe their Philadelphia buddies could ship a case of beer and have it waiting on the beach. But how could they chill it? What about some champagne? Now we were all getting into the graduation festivities, the "all-night Disneyland celebrations," the throwing of the caps into the air.

"We'll take up a collection from everyone who wants to and buy a case of champagne," I said.

"We can shake it up and squirt it around."

"Pour it on Helen's head, like they do at basketball games."

"We ought to have a band playing," suggested Barbara Haya.

"A parade," I added.

"Elephants."

"Clowns."

"Cotton candy."

But rain and winds greeted the dawn on Hampton Beach day. Marv lost his last bid to ride his bike. Even though we only had twenty miles to reach the Atlantic Ocean, Helen said the rain would make the roads dangerous. Marv would have to roll into Hampton Beach in the van.

For the rest of us it meant ponchos and abandoning our plans of Hampton Beach frivolity. Breakfast in the rain was a melancholy affair. No one had much to say. We hardly seemed aware that this was our last time to eat together. I felt depressed. This wasn't the way the ride was supposed to end.

But everyone was tired after a full evening the night before. We had given our bikes a final cleaning in the dark because we had arrived in camp late. This time I cleaned the bike myself, and actually passed Conrad's inspection.

We also had an award ceremony. Junior's distinction was having the most rebuilt parts on his bike, and Sherm's was leaving the greatest amount of skin across the country. Ed and Chip were recognized for breaking more rules than anyone else; Ted and I were cited for carrying the best "munchies" in our bike bags. Cluster two — I almost wept at this — was honored for being "the most improved cluster."

But the rain deflated us like a punctured tube. Helen, in her red rain cape, crouched on the wet basketball court near our campground to eat her cereal. The surrounding puddles on the court reflected her red to create a polka-dotted pavement, the only bright spots in a gray world. I settled under a dripping tree and tried to keep my cereal from being diluted in the rain. As I watched the design of raindrops and puddles, Barbara Haya in bright yellow crossed the court to go roll up her wet tent. Another ray of color, I thought.

Helen called us all together and asked us to bow our heads for a prayer: "We ask you, dear Lord, for the safe arrival of our group. We thank you for the friendships made. And for the accomplishment of this trip." I was next to Ted, and we squeezed each other's hand before breaking the circle.

As we walked bikes out the long gravel road to begin our final lap to the coast, I could see Ed and Chip's crepe-paper decorations and tiny American flags, soggy already. Ed blew his police whistle; Chip set off his airhorn. We were on our way.

We finally reached the highway to thread our way through the maze that led us into Massachusetts for a few miles and back to New Hampshire to the rain-soaked sign: Hampton Beach City Limits. That's it, I thought. It's all over now. My forehead felt hot under my helmet, body steaming from the poncho, and my heart was racing.

"Give me an H — give me an A — give me an M — give me a P — " Junior started the cheer.

We all took it up. "Give me a T — give me an O — give me an N — Hampton Beach. Rah, rah, rah." We turned the corner onto the beach road, and saw our waiting police escort, lights flashing and siren wailing. We rode double-file behind it to Hampton Beach. Over that noise, and Ed and Chip's whistle and horn, we sang "God Bless America" and "This Land Is Your Land." I cried and laughed. I was ecstatic.

As we crossed the last bridge to the state park at the beach, a small yellow car tried to pass the group of cyclists. Although several of us waved the car back and shouted at them, the elderly couple in the car couldn't hear us with their windows closed. They kept inching their way through our ranks.

The metal grid on the bridge, slick in the rain, caused Barbara Haya to skid. She fell.

"Stopping, stopping."

"Braking, braking." Warnings were called out as all bikers came to a halt.

The yellow car was right behind me. I kicked the bikestand down to hold my bike. My heart was pounding, and I felt a powerful sense of mission as I strode to the driver's window. "We've come four thousand miles for this," I told the man as he rolled the window down. "Please let us have this last bit of our trip all together. That's why we have the police escort."

"Sure, sure." He and his wife peered through the windshield at the fallen biker. "We didn't understand."

Barbara was back on her bike, okay, and we proceeded. I could see the ocean now, the Atlantic Ocean. The trip was completed. We had all finished the trip together after all.

The rain had stopped. Marv jumped out of the van to roll his bike with us into the surf.

A welcoming committee of family and friends surged forward, including our daughter Judy.

She had taken the day off and driven 100 miles from Springfield to meet her "crazy" parents. Her short, blond hair bounced as she ran toward us. "You made it, you made it, you made it!"

"Judy, you look great." But our family reunion became entwined with biker farewells. Kirk came up: "I'm hugging all the Barbaras," he said playfully. Michelle said goodbye to Ted and told him, "I learned a lot on this trip." I chased Junior around the parked bikes for a final hug.

I was overwhelmed. My senses were bombarded with the beach and the commotion, people waving and shouting, the Atlantic Ocean rolling up over our front bicycle wheels. Tears and promises, and the champagne.

The champagne turned out to be a problem. "There are parents here," Helen said as she asked us to move up the beach with our champagne bottle and plastic cups. "The parents might get the wrong idea." She wrinkled her nose and squinted her eyes, searching for understanding from us.

I could see her point of view. She had been responsible for these kids for almost two months; now their parents and families were observing the Out-Spokin' "graduation." Helen was in a predicament and the champagne bottle, celebration or no celebration, didn't help her any.

**The author at Hampton Beach at last, with fellow biker Craig Martin.**

"There's a picnic bench," Ted said, pointing up the beach about 100 feet. "We'll have our celebration over there."

Most in the group were winding down from their finale of exhilaration. Some were changing clothes now and cleaning up in the restrooms; others were helping disassemble bikes for the return trip. But a few were still impressed by the significance of the moment — awestruck by the occasion.

Little plastic glasses filled with bubbly liquid were lifted as a toast between mother, father, and daughter. We gazed into the mist that shrouded the sea, grinned at each other, and talked of biking adventures, Judy's trip to Yugoslavia, and how good it was to be together again — here, in this place, at this time.

I was surprised to see Helen walking up the beach toward us. "I'm sorry," she said. "I'll have to ask you to go across the street. You're still too close."

We looked across the street at the beach parking lot. There were a few cars and lots of asphalt — no sand — no redeeming features that I could see. As we talked about the situation, Helen was facing us and we could see behind her two more approaching our table. It was Ed and Chip.

They were shaking two big bottles of champagne and letting them squirt up into the air. They were laughing and running and jumping and dancing.

"I think you've got more trouble behind you," Judy laughed.

When Helen turned to view the scene, she chuckled in spite of everything. How fitting, I thought. Our community of life-and-strife is with us yet. We were still struggling with aspects of Christian freedom and responsibility right up to the last goodbye. We might have stopped pedaling at Hampton Beach, but we didn't stop being frail human beings.

Were we going to have a confrontation here on the Atlantic seacoast? Helen wanted us to move, and we wanted to stay.

I walked back to the van with Helen to get my typewriter, for we had decided to leave. She turned to me with tears glistening in her eyes. "I didn't want it to end like this," she said. "I hope this doesn't change things between us."

"Oh, no." I felt tears brimming in my own eyes as I gave her a hug. "We're still family."

Nothing could take that away, I thought. We could treasure enduring returns beyond the ride. Even though our tire tracks right now were being washed away by gentle Atlantic surf, something would remain. An invisible thread would hold us together. I knew I would anticipate news of fellow bikers' graduations, weddings, flying lessons, football victories, career launchings, and even other bike trips. Our commitment was not written in the tracked sand of Hampton Beach or made of dust to be blown away. It was made out of 3892.2 miles, founded on Solid Rock.

# CHRISTIAN HERALD ASSOCIATION AND ITS MINISTRIES

**CHRISTIAN HERALD ASSOCIATION**, founded in 1878, publishes The Christian Herald Magazine, one of the leading interdenominational religious monthlies in America. Through its wide circulation, it brings inspiring articles and the latest news of religious developments to many families. From the magazine's pages came the initiative for CHRISTIAN HERALD CHILDREN'S HOME and THE BOWERY MISSION, two individually supported not-for-profit corporations.

**CHRISTIAN HERALD CHILDREN'S HOME**, established in 1894, is the name for a unique and dynamic ministry to disadvantaged children, offering hope and opportunities which would not otherwise be available for reasons of poverty and neglect. The goal is to develop each child's potential and to demonstrate Christian compassion and understanding to children in need.

*Mont Lawn* is a permanent camp located in Bushkill, Pennsylvania. It is the focal point of a ministry which provides a healthful "vacation with a purpose" to children who without it would be confined to the streets of the city. Up to 1000 children between the ages of 7 and 11 come to Mont Lawn each year.

Christian Herald Children's Home maintains year-round contact with children by means of an *In-City Youth Ministry.* Central to its philosophy is the belief that only through sustained relationships and demonstrated concern can individual lives be truly enriched. Special emphasis is on individual guidance, spiritual and family counseling and tutoring. This follow-up ministry to inner-city children culminates for many in financial assistance toward higher education and career counseling.

**THE BOWERY MISSION**, located at 227 Bowery, New York City, has since 1879 been reaching out to the lost men on the Bowery, offering them what could be their last chance to rebuild their lives. Every man is fed, clothed and ministered to. Countless numbers have entered the 90-day residential rehabilitation program at the Bowery Mission. A concentrated ministry of counseling, medical care, nutrition therapy, Bible study and Gospel services awakens a man to spiritual renewal within himself.

These ministries are supported solely by the voluntary contributions of individuals and by legacies and bequests. Contributions are tax deductible. Checks should be made out either to CHRISTIAN HERALD CHILDREN'S HOME or to THE BOWERY MISSION.

**Administrative Office: 40 Overlook Drive, Chappaqua, New York 10514**
**Telephone: (914) 769-9000**